RESTORE

A Lost Girl's Journey to Hope

Book Two

A Memoir

TIFFANY DIONNE

CONTENTS

CHAPTER 1

"What up shorty, you lost?"

I looked up from my schedule and saw a guy walking toward me.

He grinned. "You look like you need help."

"I guess…" I was in the parking lot at school. It was my first day of 10th grade, and the light wind rustling against my arms was making me aware of my nerves.

"Can I walk you to class?" The guy took my schedule.

I pulled my backpack higher up on my shoulder, making my dress shift in the fall breeze. The air was warm, with a hint of spice in it, letting me know orange leaves would be hitting the ground soon.

I had on my best friend Tori's red and white baby doll dress. It had tiny, white flowers all over and a cinched waist. I loved the dress, and the way it accentuated my long legs down to my strapped sandals.

"Sure..." I nudged Tori's cat eyed sunglasses up against my ponytail and twirled the folds of the dress around my thumb.

What time is it?

I leaned, rocking slightly on my heel as kids rushed past me and the guy. East Kentwood was shaped like a "U" and we were standing in the center. There was a concrete lot in the middle where the teachers parked, along with the upperclassmen that were able to drive to school. Three flag poles stood guard in the middle of the drive, one for East Kentwood, one for Michigan, and a red, white, and blue flag for the U.S.

I looked around the lot, taking in the number of students coming and going. The girls looked trendier than they did in ninth grade. Instead of t-shirts and gym shoes, they had on maxi dresses and open-toed sandals, with Dooney and Bourke purses slung over their shoulders. A group of girls wore black and crimson cheer uniforms, with "EK" painted on their cheeks in red. Probably for the pep rally.

"Aggh, Shannon!" One of the girls screamed. "I've missed you!" She ran, bouncing on her toes as she hugged the girl. Glitter sparkled on her ponytail in the sunlight.

I smiled. I'd always wanted to be a cheerleader. Not trying out for the team was one of my big regrets.

I had a lot of regrets.

I played with the strap on my purse as the parking lot buzzed with first-day energy … and jitters from not knowing what to expect on the huge campus.

The guys looked bulkier than they did the year before. Their shoulders were square and their necks were wide, like they'd been lifting weights. A group of them strolled past us, jokingly shoving each other. They had on letterman jackets with our falcon mascot emblazoned on the back. There was a confidence in how they pushed through the busy lot with their chests leading the way. They must have been on the football team.

I held my hand over my eyes to block the sun out. I only had a few minutes before I'd be late for class.

"Let's see…" The guy ran his finger across my paper. He had a swag about him that I liked. He was a little shorter than me, he reminded me of this rapper I listened to. They had the same dark complexion and bald head. His chiseled features would have fit perfectly in the background of one of my favorite artist's videos.

"You were lost, huh?" He grabbed my backpack. "I got that…"

It was my first day on the main campus. East Kentwood was big. We had our own building in ninth grade. There were at least 700 freshmen. Every time I pulled up to my school I thought about how it looked more like a university than a high school, from the olympic-sized pool to the ice skating rink that I hoped I would finally be able to try out.

"Follow me." The guy threw his head up.

I drummed my fingers across the smooth leather of my purse as we walked. I was looking forward to being in the older building. I'd felt like I was suffocating in ninth grade.

A new atmosphere will make things better.

I needed something new.

I'd stopped hanging with Hannah and broke up with David in the summertime. I didn't want to deal with either of them. Hannah was too much trouble, and David tried too hard to act like he cared, and I didn't want to be bothered with anybody trying to love me. I'd loved Gideon, and that didn't work.

Even if nothing had happened that night at the prayer meeting, things had changed.

I followed the guy, thinking about how sophomore year was going to be different. I hadn't changed much physically, I was still arms and legs, or "statuesque" like Mom called me when I was little and I would get self-conscious about my height. My amber skin still shone in the sun. I wore my ponytail a little higher than the year before, but besides that, things on the outside were the same. Inside, everything was different.

Dad had moved to Arizona.

That was what he had wanted to talk to me about in front of Mom's apartment.

Things haven't been right for a while now, I remembered him saying.

That day changed the world. He'd run out of engineering contracts and said he had to leave.

I was devastated. I was used to my cousins, Serena and Sam, visiting in the summertime, and hanging out with Tori at Dad's house from Friday night to Sunday afternoon when everyone else was getting out of church. When he told me he was leaving I went in the house and hid in the bathroom. I wanted to cry, but the tears wouldn't fall.

Dad had always been there, fussing at me and Tori, telling us to be good people, taking us places he said would enlighten our minds, like the Museum of Natural Arts and History in Chicago, or the planetarium; with him gone none of the things I was used to could happen. I didn't have little things Mom couldn't afford, like hair supplies, or extra cash for Hungry Howie's Pizza after school. I didn't feel right asking for field trip money, if there was a scheduled trip I'd wait until after my permission slip was due and act like I forgot to return it. I didn't feel right asking for nail polish remover, or small things like socks.

Mom had shown me how to sew up my old socks that had holes in them from being worn out, but I never did because I hated the feel of crooked seams on my toes.

I hadn't felt right asking for anything after getting back from Texas.

"Nobody told your mother to leave!" Dad would say when he went off on a rant about Mom. *"I don't give a dab-blame what the court says, I'm not paying them to split up my family! This is your mother's doing. I told that woman not to take you out of my house!"*

He'd karate chop his hand, mad, like the day he'd ripped up their agreement when he picked me up after Mom took me. I'd nod from the passenger seat of our station wagon like I hadn't heard it before.

"If it wasn't for your mother I'd have jobs - good jobs. You can come live with me anytime you want to. You can come live with me right now! Under no uncertain terms will I pay those crooks one red cent..."

Dad said he would visit. I knew he would because he always did what he said, but I was hurt. The day he said he was leaving was the worst day of my life.

I acted like I didn't care, but I felt like I was bleeding inside. All that fighting he did to get me — Mom kidnapping me and him fighting to get me back, just to leave. That's what everybody did.

Gideon had disappeared after freshman year.

After convincing me I was his girl, even though he was seven years older than me, he stopped showing up.

I was in shock. I hated Gideon, but at the same time I loved him, and that made no sense. I had gotten used to him coming over every Wednesday, and the way he would force himself on me. It wasn't fair. How could he be there one day, then turn around and never come back? I didn't ask him to be my boyfriend. He was the one who said we were together.

Maybe he'd gotten bored … or maybe coming all the way to Mom's house was an inconvenience. I knew he was mad when I didn't move into Breton Court with Dad like I told him I was going to, but that wasn't a good enough reason to disappear.

Maybe he decided to build a family with his new baby.

I smoothed my flyaways into my ponytail as I followed the guy across the parking lot. "Hey girl," I waved at a familiar face.

"Hey, Tiff!" Monique took her headphones off and waved back. Her hair was in microbraids like the singer, Brandy, and she wore a flowy, bohemian dress with a faded, vintage backpack draped over her arm. She had on big gold earrings and body jewelry around her waist; they matched her laid back personality, perfectly. I admired her style. Monique got along with everyone. She was one of those girls that would hug you in the morning before class and tell you to have a great day, and mean it. I wished I could be as comfortable as she was in her skin. Her coppery, nutmeg skin tone was my favorite characteristic of hers. I liked my own shade of brown too, but my favorite feature of mine was my freckles. Most people didn't know I had them. They were one of those features that people saw without "seeing." I'd started wearing foundation in the summer, but the butterscotch freckles splashed across my nose still shone through enough for people who had known me for a long time to stop mid-sentence and squint.

"What's up with you, girl?" The guy showing me to class bopped through the mob of students, tipping two fingers towards Monique in a salute.

"Hey, you!" Monique waved, keeping up with the crowd. "It's been a while, I'll check you two out later, ok?"

"See you later." I went back to my thoughts about

the past year. The idea of Gideon being with someone other than me made my chest hurt.

I'd *thought* I was his girlfriend, that was the reason I'd put up with him treating me like I didn't exist, and him having sex with me when I didn't want to. But his real girlfriend was the one he'd had the baby by. I didn't know about her until after his son was born.

I'd never asked Gideon questions, even when he would go MIA. I was too scared. He was grown. She was the one he'd stopped coming over for, for weeks, then picked back up like nothing had happened. She might have been the reason he disappeared for good. Or he found somebody he liked better. Someone younger, or more experienced and who knew what he wanted them to do.

I had wanted to be upset about Gideon leaving me behind, but I couldn't. I didn't want to crumble. I didn't feel like I deserved to care one way or the other. The pain that tried to find its way into my subconscious was embarrassing to me. Gideon didn't care about me, so I shouldn't have let myself feel anything for him. I was stupid for thinking he liked me. I was just a girl he had used, I wasn't supposed to fall in love. I couldn't feel anything but the ache in my heart that wouldn't go away.

I sighed. I hated thinking about Gideon.

I loved him — or I *felt* like I loved him. Ever since I'd gotten taken, things in my heart were flipped upside down. Right was wrong and wrong was right, and I didn't know if I knew what love was anymore.

There was a hole in my heart.

I swept my bangs to the side and adjusted Tori's glasses.

Maybe I'll get more involved in school…

The thought cheered me up.

I liked sports. I ran track in middle school. I always placed in hurdles and long jump. Mom said I was a natural because of my long legs. The feeling of the wind against my skin was an adrenaline boost. I'd tip my head back and run until it felt like I was floating and I could leave my fears behind. East Kentwood had tons of extra-curricular activities but I hadn't participated, I'd spent all ninth grade dealing with Gideon and his boys. Since I'd met him I hadn't done anything like a regular teenager would.

That was freshman year. Gideon being gone had given me a chance to think. I *had* changed. I was tired of giving in to what people wanted. I'd made a vow to myself that things would be different after I got over the fact that Dad had left.

Summertime was off the hook.

Mom had moved us into Camelot at the end of ninth grade. Camelot was a low-income housing complex where the rent was based on how much money you made. The projects. *Everybody* lived there. There were chicks with no job and two kids, and their rent was $45 a month. Camelot was off the chain. There was nothing but single mothers, boyfriends, drug dealers, and kids. It had a park that was always packed, and a basketball court that filled up in the evening like the one at Dad's old apartment.

In the summertime mosquitoes buzzed in the street lamps, almost as loud as the hum from the chicks on their porches yelling at their kids and gossiping. I got a kick out of how live things were after living in Kentwood. The suburbs were boring.

Tori and her mom had moved into Camelot when I was in 3rd grade. Mom had put in an application to get us on the waiting list when she first got back from Texas. We moved in as soon as her name came up. It wasn't ghetto, just hood. The townhouses were nice, and there was a lot of space for kids to play.

Mom got a job working around the corner at a retirement community. She said it felt like she could breathe again after struggling for so long to pay the bills. I was excited to be around so many teenagers my age. Living close to Tori was the icing on the cake for me. I thought I would never see her again when I was in Texas, now I could walk around the corner to her house.

I was already cool with Tori's friends from when I would stay the night, but once I moved into Camelot we were inseparable. We would take all day getting dressed, go up to the courts, walk to the mall, or go out to eat. Everything was within walking distance. Our group consisted of me, Tori, Shonda, Brianne, and Shae. They were more like my sisters than my friends. They were all three to four years older than me.

I *had* changed.

Just not how I was supposed to.

I messed with this guy named Chris that lived around the corner. I was cool with his sister, but he and I had hardly ever hung out. He asked me to come chill with him one day. I didn't even like him, but I ended up going, and we kicked it in the basement. I had sex with him, just because.

I met Ronnie one day when I stayed the night at Tori's house. Me and Ronnie started kickin' it over the phone, and it was on after that. He was a Cass Avenue boy. Cass was a street in the city that everybody looked at like a gang. His house was just beyond an abandoned parking lot that had more broken glass in it than cars, and where teenagers would stay out half the night playing basketball until it got too late for the police not to mess with them. It seemed like a dark cloud hung over Ronnie's neighborhood. Like the kids there would never have enough, kinda like me. He would call me a cab and have me ditch it at his boys' house so we could kick it. I'd tell Mom I was staying the night at Tori's so she wouldn't wonder where I was.

Ronnie was *fine*. He had cinnamon brown skin with a hint of red in it. His dimples were so deep I'd get lost in his smile whenever he'd laugh. He was smart, but all he did was sell weed and smoke. He was put on house arrest for getting caught selling halfway through the summer. I would visit him at his grandmother's house, but after a while I started hearing about him messing with other chicks, so I backed off.

I went to middle school with Mark. His sister had her own place down the street from me. He spent the summer with her so he could be closer to his friends that lived in Camelot. He'd call after his sister put her kids to bed and let me know when it was okay to come over. I'd listen at the bottom of the steps before leaving the house; Mom would be in her room with the television turned down low, listening to TBN while she fell asleep. Her TV stayed on the Christian station.

After making sure Mom wasn't paying attention

I'd leave. The air would be sticky during the walk to Mark's sister's house at dusk, the most humid part of the day. Little kids would be going inside for the night and the adults and teenagers would replace them at the basketball court. I'd stay gone for hours and be back home before Mom knew I was gone. Me and Mark had sex and drank, on repeat, all summer. His sister would get me Fuzzy Navel Boone's Farm, and Mark would drink shots of E&J straight out the bottle. I'd get tore up off a couple sips. Tori had always called me a lightweight. One night Mark looked at me weird.

"Don't you think we should be together?"

" 'Be together,' like what?"

"Like, kick it."

I put my shoes on to leave. *"No..."*

"Why?" His jaw tightened, shifting back and forth. He narrowed his eyes. *"That's what people do when they like each other."*

Mark didn't understand how I could sleep with him and not want to be in a relationship. We had been messing around like that for a long time. I had never been like that before. He knew middle school Tiffany. That version of me was gone. He kept asking me to be with him, but I didn't want him getting close. I didn't trust him. I didn't trust *anyone*. I didn't want my heart getting involved with anyone ever again. I figured if I didn't feel anything for the guys I was messing with they couldn't hurt me.

That was over the summer.

I cut everybody off before school started. Gideon was gone and I didn't want to blame my actions on him. I didn't want a reputation. Part of me really did want to change for good. I acted cold, but I was hurt because the most important people in my life had betrayed me. I wanted to be better, I just didn't know if I could.

"What's your name?" The guy looked over his shoulder as we cut across the parking lot.

"Tiffany."

"Pretty. Miss. Tiffany." He grinned. "My name's Julian."

"Nice meeting you."

"It's nice to meet you, too." Julian stopped and gave this guy a play. "What up bro, I ain't seen you all summer..."

Dude slapped his hand and leaned into a hug. "What's up, Julian?"

"Nothin' much, just doin' this school thing."

"I feel you..."

"No doubt," Julian threw up his head, walking backwards. "You been in the studio?"

"Not lately. We gon' have to go lay down some tracks."

"Fa sho'." Julian grinned, pointing at him. "You better get to class, bro. You runnin' late."

"You crazy…" Dude laughed.

"I'mma check you out at lunch," Julian snapped. "One."

Julian swerved to get out of the way of traffic going towards the west wing. He couldn't get two feet without stopping to speak to somebody. We reached the door, and he held it open as the smell of hamburgers greeted us.

"The cafeteria is over there." He pointed to a room full of tables. "It's smaller than the one in the east wing, but most of your classes are on this side…"

I smiled at how he walked with a bounce in his step. Like he had music playing in his ears.

"It's quicker to come through the parking lot than the building…" he said as we stepped into the foyer. "… you'll get the hang of it after a couple days." I felt his gaze on me as I walked through the door ahead of him.

I let Julian take the lead as we turned down the hall.

He's kinda cute, I thought.

Julian pulled my schedule back out and stopped outside a door with kids rushing to get to their seats. "Here you go." He looked at the clock on the wall outside the classroom and shot me a crooked grin. "I got you here on time, too."

"Thanks, I would have still been looking for it."

"No problem." He slid my backpack off his shoulder and handed it to me.

I looked at him warily. "Aren't you going to be late?"

"Nah...all the teachers know me around here."

I giggled. "What's that got to do with you being late?"

A tall man, who I guessed was my teacher, walked towards us, greeting the last few students coming into the room.

"What up, Mr. Delaney!" Julian called over my shoulder.

"Julian! Long time no see." Mr. Delaney patted him on the back. "You're not in my class. What are you doing on this side of campus?"

Julian motioned towards me. "You know me, just helping out a friend."

My teacher smiled. "Good man..." He nodded at the wall. "Just make sure you keep an eye on the clock."

Julian gave him a pound. "Good lookin' out, sir."

I shook my head as Mr. Delaney went back to his desk. "You do know everybody."

"I told you." He said with a twinkle in his eye.

I looked around the room. The empty chairs were filling up. "Thank you for walking me..."

"You're welcome." He stepped aside for one of my classmates. "Aye, we should exchange numbers before you go." He winked. "Just in case you ever need help."

CHAPTER 2

"So, can I come see you?" It was Friday afternoon and Julian and I had been on the phone since we got out of school. He had called every night that week. "Yeah, if you want."

"Cool, I'mma holla at you around 7:00."

I ran up the steps to see what I was going to wear. I was excited to see Julian outside of school. I wasn't sure if I was feeling him yet, I wasn't trying to get distracted one week into the school year, but I liked his attention. I could tell Julian was different. I wanted something new.

I looked through my closet. Luckily me and Tori traded clothes so our wardrobes would look bigger than what they were. I pulled a white tennis skirt off my top shelf and held it against my waist.

"Uh-uh…" I wrinkled up my nose and put it back. The skirt was shorter than I'd remembered and I didn't want to look like I was trying too hard. I took a pink dress off its hanger and threw it on my bed.

After I found Tori's blue slingback sandals in the back of my closet I jumped in the shower to wash my hair. I let water run over me as I poured body wash onto my towel. It smelled like a mix of peaches, honey, and oats. I didn't like the smell of peaches. Mom had been given the fancy glass bottle as a gift. I'd swirl the white and blush contents around the jar when I sat in the bathtub in the morning before school. The colors reminded me of the ribbons Mom used to put in my hair when I was little. How she used to get me dressed for church.

I shook my head, chasing the memory away. The sweet smell of the body wash got on my nerves, but I knew Mom wasn't going to buy new soap until the jar was empty. I wrung out my hair as I turned off the water and got out of the bath.

It shouldn't be so dark, I thought as I stepped out onto the square rug. I flicked the bathroom light switch. Nothing.

"Mom?" I called from the doorway.

I fumbled for the cocoa butter I'd left on the counter.

"Mom?"

I cussed as Mom's big jar of Vaseline fell into the sink.

Good thing it didn't fall on my foot.

"Ma?" I found my vanilla body splash and sprayed my damp skin. I wondered if Julian would like the smell. I had to hurry before he showed up. It was almost 7:00. My hair took a long time to do.

"Mom!" I yelled into the hall.

The house was black and the echo from my voice was giving me goosebumps.

I wrapped myself in a towel and went room to room, flicking on each light.

Don't let the power be out.

"Mom?"

She must already be at church. She went to prayer on Fridays.

I paused at my door and tried the light in my room.

Dang …

I reached for my hair. It was already starting to shrivel up. I snatched off my towel and threw it into the pile of dirty clothes.

***

"Hey," I answered the door, smashing down my hair. "Don't look at my head…the power went out, and I couldn't blow dry my hair before you—"

Julian pulled one of my tight naps. "Chill out, I like it." He stepped back, taking in the springy hair that had started to frame my face.

"Yeah right …"

Julian grinned. "It's pretty, just like you."

I took a deep breath and stepped onto the porch.

"What's your favorite color?" He asked.

I eyed him as I sat down. "Turquoise."

Julian's eyes lit up. "For real?"

It was my first time really looking him in his eyes over the past week of talking on the phone. They were a deep brown with a bright ring of chestnut around the edge.

"Why? Is it yours too?"

"Naw, mines is green, but it's close."

"You are silly."

Julian ran his hand across my arm like he was

smoothing out any leftover nerves. "You like going to the movies?"

"Yeah."

"Bet, I'm a movie head. What's your favorite?"

"You go first."

"Naw, then you ain't gon' tell me your favorite."

"I promise I'll tell you."

"Alright," Julian looked up. " I'm old school. I like stuff like *Star Wars, Star Trek...*"

"*Star Wars?*"

"You don't like *Star Wars?*"

"I *hate Star Wars.*"

"Aww man, don't tell me that. We gon' have to have a *Star Wars* marathon when you come to the house."

I leaned on him, laughing. "That sounds boring." I'd get upset when my brothers would watch *Star Wars.* The movies were long, and I didn't understand them. They'd get in arguments with my uncles about which one they thought was the best.

"No it doesn't. You don't know what you've been missing out on."

"I'm fine missing out."

"Your turn." Julian said.

"Don't laugh."

He shot me a wounded look. "What makes you think I would laugh?"

I eyed him.

"Come on, you agreed."

I blushed, focusing on the treeline beyond the big field that separated Camelot from the main road. "Alright," I turned back. *The Sound of Music.*

Watching musicals was a tradition for me and Dad. He would say, *"People who take an interest in music are intelligent people..."* He would make me, Garret, Nigel and Rodney watch musicals like *Fiddler on the Roof* and *West Side Story.* My brothers hated it, but I didn't mind.

We got a VCR when I was seven. *The Sound of Music* was the first video we rented.

"We can put our movies here!" I exclaimed, pointing to the hollow cubby in Mom and Dad's dresser the first time we got home from the video store.

I had watched *The Sound of Music* over and over. After I was taken it made me feel good to watch movies me and Dad used to like. I'd stop what I was doing to watch them when they came on regular television, even if no one else was there.

"*The Sound of Music?*" Julian said, cracking up.

"Don't laugh at me!"

"I'm not." He grabbed my arm. "I'm not laughing at you … I'm laughing with you."

I punched him in his shoulder. "No you're not."

Julian took my hand. "For real though, I just didn't take you for the musical type, but they're cool."

I shook my head, "It's just something between me and my Dad. Have you seen *The Sound of Music?*"

His eyes sparkled. "Nope."

"You should watch it."

"Naw, I don't think so."

"Hmph, well, if you watch *The Sound of Music* with me, I'll watch *Star Wars.*"

"Aww, man…" Julian palmed his head. "What I get myself into?"

I giggled.

It was silly, but watching old movies made me feel safe. Like how comfortable things were before I was gone, before Dad had that faraway look in his eyes whenever he spoke about our family.

Me and Julian talked for the next hour. He was a junior, one grade above me. He was a goofball. Every other word out of his mouth had me laughing. We talked about school and our friends. I told him how close me and Tori were. He told me about his boys. His best friend, Curtis, went to East Kentwood with us.

The wind picked up and made me shiver.

"You cold?" Julian asked.

"A little … I would say let's go inside, but my mom don't like guys being in the house when she's not home."

Julian ran his thumb across my chin. "I'm cool sitting out here with you."

I felt my cheeks getting hot. I thought about Gideon — how opposite from Julian he was. Gideon would have never sat on the porch, talking. All he'd ever wanted was sex. He never came around without forcing himself on me. It was hard to believe all Julian wanted to do was hang out with me. Panic crept into my chest as I tried to think of something to say.

"Moms should be pulling up any second." Julian nudged me. "I had fun."

"Me too."

"Yeah? Well I don't wanna go back to school on Monday the same."

I screwed up my face. "The same as what?"

Julian looked at me intently. "I don't wanna be your friend on Monday."

I narrowed my eyes as he paused.

"...I wanna be your man."

"You are *silly*."

He grinned. "Is that a yes?"

I blushed. I liked Julian. He wasn't the type of guy that usually hollered at me, I wasn't thinking about hooking up with anyone so soon. I had wanted to be different than I was over the last year. I didn't think I was ready to date. I wasn't used to talking to high school boys. I'd thought I would always want to be with somebody older, like Gideon. It was weird liking someone my age. Julian made me feel comfortable. I couldn't ever remember feeling "right" with a boy, but I felt right with him.

"Mmm," I looked at my hands. "It's a yes."

He leaned forward and kissed me on my temple. "Cool."

Maybe I don't know my type.

A burgundy car pulled into the circular drive and honked.

"Come meet Moms." Julian pulled me to my feet.

He palmed my hand as we walked to the car. "Hey Ma," He leaned into the window, motioning toward me, "This my new girlfriend."

"Girlfriend?" His mother's eyes sparkled. "Julian, I didn't know you like girls with afros."

"Ma!"

I reached up. I'd forgotten about how jacked up my hair looked from not being able to blow dry it.

"I'm playin' boy." She turned towards me. "It's nice to meet you…"

Butterflies danced in my stomach. I was excited to have a new boyfriend. I was also scared.

I hope I've changed…

CHAPTER 3

"Let me carry that for you, bae…" Julian reached for my backpack. "Whatchu got in here? Like, a hundred books?"

I bumped him playfully. "You're just not used to having your books."

"That's what happens when you're cool with the teachers." He nudged my chin.

"You need to get cool with them books." I laughed.

We were in front of the cafeteria's big glass windows where everyone met in-between classes. It was only second period, but I could already smell the salt from the french fries.

One of Julian's boys gave him a pound. "Your girl got you carrying bags, bro? She got you whipped already."

"Ohhhhh," The hallway erupted in laughter.

Julian threw up his head. "Aye bro, you wish you *had* a girl so you *could* carry a bag."

"*Ohhhhhhhhhh...*"

Julian's best friend, Curtis, slapped the guy's shoulder playfully. "He said, 'you *wish* you had a girl!' "

Julian gave Curtis a play. "What's wrong with this fool?" He jammed his thumb in dude's direction. "I'mma always carry my girl's stuff."

Curtis nodded.

I covered my mouth to hide my laugh. Me and Julian had been kickin' it for a couple weeks. He walked me to every class and knew my schedule by heart. We were together all day at school and spent hours at night on the phone. We'd talk about our family and each other's favorite things. He loved East Coast rappers and thought mainstream music was wack. And he loved coming up with new beats. I'd tell him about class and what Tori and our friends were getting into in Camelot. I'd never had a guy pay me so much attention. I was having fun being with Julian, but it was awkward sometimes. I wondered what he liked about me.

"So y'all official?" Curtis asked Julian.

"Yeah, bro, that's my shorty"

My girl Lisa leaned on me. "You guys are cute, Tiff."

"Thanks girl." I wrinkled up my nose. "It's only been a few weeks, though." I downplayed how much I liked Julian to my friends. I didn't want to get used to the idea of having a boyfriend at school if things didn't work out.

"Girl, so what." Lisa eyed me like I was crazy. "School just started and you already got a man? Same ol' Tiff…"

"It's not even like that…" I hated when my girls talked about how many guys I'd kicked it with. I'd only started having real boyfriends the year before, but it seemed like I'd already had so many I couldn't keep track of them all. I didn't want people thinking I had a reputation at East Kentwood.

"Hmph," Lisa pouted. "I wish I had a boyfriend to carry my bags."

"You so stupid," I laughed, pushing her off my shoulder.

"You scooped her up, quick." Curtis said.

Julian jabbed at him. "I couldn't let none of y'all knuckleheads get at her."

"Man, right out of the Freshman campus…"

Julian put his fist over his mouth. "I'm tellin' you."

I narrowed my eyes. "Bae."

"Them freshmen chicks be pretty…"

"Bae." I let the word linger, like I couldn't believe I was the topic of their conversation.

"What's up?" Julian's eyes danced with mine, he smiled, showing his full set of perfect teeth.

I turned so he wouldn't see me blush. "Come on…" I wondered if he knew he had that effect on me. The way he talked about me made my cheeks hurt from trying to hide my smile. I'd never had a boy like me so much. Especially not one I liked back. Julian was so goofy, I wondered if he was being serious when he talked about us.

"What's up, boo?" Julian teased.

I looked at Lisa. "They just gon' talk about me like I'm not here?"

"I know." Lisa laughed.

"She *is* cute…" Curtis said.

Julian shrugged. "Man, my girl is *fine*…"

"I see you." One of his boys nodded his agreement, looking down the length of my body.

"Hey, hey," Julian's eyebrows knit together as he

stuck his arm in front of me and pushed me gently back.

"Julian…"

The guys doubled over.

"Man, ain't nobody trying to get with your girl."

Julian huffed, "Yeah, alright." He tried keeping the mock seriousness in his tone. "Let's keep it that way."

"*Man* Julian," Jackson threw his head back. "You crazy."

I shook my head as Julian gave Jackson a pound, and they both cracked up.

Lisa shoved him playfully, "You a mess."

Jackson held his stomach from clowning his friend. He was a junior. We had 3rd period trigonometry together on the opposite side of the building. He would ask how things were going with Julian every day after lunch when he'd dropped his Tommy Hifiger backpack in front of my desk. Sometimes I thought Jackson had a crush on me. He had deep dimples and the prettiest smile that he was always flashing at girls, like they were supposed to melt. I would never talk to him. He was a player.

He was always telling me his business about some girl that liked him, but he wasn't sure if he liked her back. I would shake my head while finishing up my work. Dating was a game to Jackson, the way he talked and how girls fell all over him reminded me of Gideon's cousin, Brandon. I wasn't going to be another chic on his list.

I put my hand on my hip. "Babe."

"What's up, boo?" Julian reached for me.

"You so silly, I gotta get to my class."

"I'mma walk you, boo, I'm just tryna make sure these fools know what's up."

"Got to," Curtis nodded.

"Bae."

"What?" Julian shrugged. "If I don't do it, who else will?"

"Boy, you are crazy."

"You my bae, though…"

"Julian, if you don't come on." I laughed.

"I'm coming bae, just let me—"

Lisa fell out laughing. "Julian, you are nuts."

He smiled wider. "Come here, bae." He held out his hand to me.

"Uh-uh," I stepped back, shaking my head. "You might not care about your grades, but I do. Come on Lisa," I looped my arm through hers.

"But, bae…"

"No!" I turned away from Julian, giggling. "The bell is about to ring."

"Bae, I just need to— "

"Julian."

"Alright, alright, alright." He stepped in front of me and took my hand. "I'm messing with you, bae." He leaned forward, nudging one of the guys with his shoulder and pointing at his boy on the football team. "Let me get my girl to class, I'll check y'all out later."

"Do your thing," Curtis slapped his hand. "I'll holla at you at lunch."

Julian snapped. "One."

✳✳✳

"Julian?" I lay on my back, running my hands across the slats underneath the bunk bed he shared with his little brother.

"What's up, bae?"

"Nothing."

He pinched my side. "Why you calling me then?"

"I dunno," I smiled. "Because I can."

I had been at Julian's house for the last hour. We were in his room letting our food digest.

Julian leaned into my neck. "You lucky I like you."

"Stop," I swat him away, giggling from the way his breath tickled the corner of my ear. I inhaled. I loved the way Julian smelled. A mix of wood, musk, and the Carmex he'd put on his lips at school every couple hours. I could almost taste the tingly mint before he would kiss me.

Julian blew in my ear.

"Stop!" I leaned into his pillow and kicked my legs up. Julian had an ease about him. Like he was always sharing an inside joke. I felt like we'd known each other for years.

"You guys—" Tyrell, Julian's little brother, burst into the room.

"Get out!" Julian yelled.

"I don't have to." Tyrell looked offended. "This my room, too."

Tyrell was dark skinned and chunky. His hair rolled up into tight curls, even though Julian was always telling him to brush it.

"Tyrell, what I say?" Julian sat up on the bed.

Tyrell narrowed his eyes. "I'm telling Mom you got Tiffany in here with the door closed."

"We ain't' even doing nothing, punk. Leave."

"Ma!" Tyrell called over his shoulder.

"You get on my nerves, with your fat self."

Julian's mom called up the steps. "Tyrell, what do you want?"

"Julian called me fat, and he's up here with the door closed when he knows he's not supposed to be."

"Get. Out!"

"Julian, open up that door!"

I looked between the two of them, amused at how Tyrell had Julian so upset.

"It's open, Ma! Can you tell Tyrell to get outta here?"

"Tyrell, bring your butt down them steps." Their mom said. "They don't want you up there messing with them."

I laughed. I wished my brothers were still home. I missed listening to them talk after school while they did their chores, or how I'd eavesdrop on their conversations when I was supposed to be asleep.

"Tiffany," Tyrell turned back to us. "Can we play Uno?"

I smiled. "Sure."

"*Yes,*" He pumped his fist like he'd won a prize.

"Can you go find the cards?" I asked.

"How long?"

I looked at the clock on their nightstand. "Give me half an hour.

"Ok, I'll be back." He glared at Julian. "And y'all better keep the door open. Don't be trying to have sex in my room."

I covered my mouth.

"Aye, man..." Julian grabbed a book off the floor and threw it at Tyrell's shoulder.

"Ma!" Tyrell took off, laughing. "He's still messing with me!"

"Punk."

I buried my head in Julian's pillow. "No he did not..."

"Chump. Gets on my nerves..."

I giggled.

Tyrell was sweet. He was only in 5th grade. I wished I had a brother that was closer in age to me. I thought about how Rodney would never let me win when we played Uno. I missed Rodney. He was away at college.

Julian laid back on the bed and propped his head up with his arms. "You think we gon' be together for a long time?"

I hesitated. "What made you ask that?"

"Cuz, I want us to…"

I looked back up at the bed slats and let my knuckles graze the rough wood. "Yeah."

"That's good." He wrapped his arm around me and leaned sleepily into my chest.

"You better quit before Tyrell comes back and sees you laying on me."

Julian smirked. "Don't nobody care about Tyrell."

"Leave him alone."

"Nah, that's my little homie. He only acts like that cuz he likes you."

I smiled. I enjoyed being around Julian's family. His

mom had made fried chicken, mashed potatoes, green beans, and a salad for dinner. When we sat down she had Julian pour me a cup of purple Kool-Aid. Mom never bought Kool-Aid. She said all that sugar wasn't good for you.

Julian's mom had picked me up that afternoon when they got out of church. Their house was peaceful. My house was more quiet than peaceful, being at home for too long made me sad. I felt like the walls were caving in on me. I was still making everyone around me unhappy. Mom and Dad fought over me so hard, but they were both still sad when I was right in front of them. I loved being at Julian's house. His family seemed happy to have me around.

I took Julian's hand and held it up over my head.

He opened his eyes. "Why you keep messing with me?"

"Cuz, I want you to wake up."

"I ate too much, bae, I need a nap."

"Nooo, talk to me."

"I am talking to you." He smiled.

"You know what I mean."

"Ok." Julian kissed me. "What do you want to talk

about?"

"Anything. I don't care."

He closed his eyes like he was starting to doze again.

"Bae."

"I'm not asleep."

"Ok. Tell me something."

"Tell you what?"

"Tell me something I don't know."

"Alright…" Julian paused with his eyes shut and I took in his high cheekbones and dark, mahogany skin. I ran my hand across the stubble on his chin and traced the sharp lines of his face. I loved the shape of his bald head and the way his nose flared when he was trying to figure something out.

I pulled on his ear.

"Stop, bae…"

"You're falling asleep."

"No I'm not. I'm thinking about what I should tell you." Julian opened his eyes and stared, like he was seeing me for the first time.

"What?" The look on his face made me feel

self-conscious. Like he could see inside of me.

He drew the corner of his lip into his mouth.

"What?"

Julian hesitated. "I think I'm falling in love with you."

My heartbeat thumped in my ears as my breath caught in my chest.

He thinks he loves me?

He smiled. "Was that something you wanted to hear?"

My voice dropped to a whisper. "I guess so…"

"Good." He closed his eyes. The lazy curve of his smile made him look content.

He thinks he loves me.

Warmth built up inside me, spilling over to my face. Love. Had a guy ever loved me? I'd been in love. I loved my Dad. I loved my brothers. I'd loved Gideon.

I wanted to run away. I felt guilty inside.

CHAPTER 4

"*Tiff-anyyy.*" Mom came into the living room.

"What?" I looked up from my homework. She smelled good. Like the broccoli and potato soup she'd been making.

She frowned. "Don't answer mama like that."

I put my pencil down and sighed.

"Whatchu working on?" She picked up one of my folders.

"Nothin'."

She waved her hand over the books and papers laid out on the couch. "This looks like a whole lotta somethin' to me." She chuckled.

"Just some science." I had a lot of homework to do, but I didn't feel like telling Mom about it. I wanted her to hurry up and say what she had to say.

"How's Julian?" She thumbed through my notebook.

"Fine."

"Just fine?" She'd met him twice since we'd been kickin' it, but she heard us talking on the phone.

"Mmmhmm..." I slid my English folder into my backpack.

"What grade is he in again?"

"— Eleventh."

"Hmm, that's not too bad. What kind of things does he like to do?"

I looked up. Ever since I'd gotten taken it was hard for me to talk to Mom. I wasn't trying to get smart with her. I knew I shouldn't be disrespectful. I just couldn't connect with her trying to dig into my life. Ever since getting taken to Texas I'd had a wall up. "I don't know, Mom."

"Seems like you should know if you go together. What do you like about him?"

"Mom," I breathed hard.

"What? I just want to know something about him."

"He likes the same things I like. He likes rapping and music."

"Rapping?" Her brows scrunched up.

"See? I shouldn't have told you anything."

"I didn't say anything bad. Rapping? What kind of rapping? Like, gangster rapping? "

I put my hand on my head. "Nooo…"

She held her hands up, "Well, I don't know. Tell me what kind of *rapping* Mr. Julian likes."

"Just rapping, Mom. He likes music and making beats."

"Ok." She paused. "Don't you think you should take things slow, not have a boyfriend again so quick?"

I stopped shuffling my papers. "No."

"Well, the last time you had a breakup you took it hard. Don't you think you should slow things down?"

Mom was thinking about Jericho. She didn't know what she was talking about. He wasn't my last boyfriend. He was the last guy she'd seen me cry over. It had taken me months to get over him, but he wasn't the last guy I'd been with. Gideon was way worse.

I shook my head. "I'll be fine."

"Well," Mom put on her perky voice. "Tell me one thing you like about Julian."

"Mom." I groaned.

"Come on, just one thing. There's gotta be something you like."

"There is, I just can't think of it."

She held up a finger. "Just one thing."

I laughed. "He's nice."

"He's nice? You can do better than that."

"Mom."

"Come on…"

"Ok, he's nice and he's funny."

"He's funny? That's good. I like to laugh." She chuckled.

"Yeah, well, he's funny."

"Does he do well in school?"

"I don't know." Julian did horrible in school from what I'd seen. The only reason he was passing was because teachers liked him. Or because one of his classmates let him copy their work.

"Well, as much as you two are on the phone I hope so, or else his grades are going to be in the pits."

"Mom…"

"I'm just saying. Don't you think the two of you talk on the phone too much?"

"No."

"Well I do. You don't want to spend too much time on boys right now. Spend more time getting to know the Lord. That'll keep you grounded."

I tried not to roll my eyes. I knew she was going to have something negative to say.

"Don't make that face. Mama's being serious because I care about you. I don't want you getting distracted and forgetting about the things that are important. You spend time with God and you'll always do well. You focus all your attention on boys and who knows what'll come of those relationships. You gotta stay grounded."

I nodded. "Ok Mom."

"Are you saying 'ok Mom' just to pacify me?"

"No."

"Hmm, does Julian believe in God?"

I clicked my tongue against the roof of my mouth. "I think..."

"Well, that's one thing you know you need to be figuring out."

I breathed out hard. This was why I hated talking to Mom. All of our conversations circled back to God and what I should be doing. I really didn't know what Julian believed. I knew he went to church on Sundays, but we didn't talk about God like that.

"You understand where mama's coming from, right?"

I pursed my lips. "Yeah."

"Mama, just cares about you. I don't want you getting hurt. I love you."

***

"What's up, bae?"

"Hey." I opened the door wide for Julian to come in.

He pecked me on the cheek and brushed past me into the hallway. "You doing alright?" He took his boots off.

"I'm cool." I leaned out the door to wave goodbye to his mom, then hung up his coat.

We went into the living room and plopped down on the sofa.

"I'm glad I'm here." He put his arm around me and

I leaned into his chest. Julian cupped my head in the crook of his elbow and smacked a kiss on my cheek.

"...so silly." I nudged him with my forehead.

He smiled. "You smell good."

"Thanks." I looked at the television. Only the corner lamp in the living room was on. The room had a dim orange glow as the sun went down outside. I didn't know why I was nervous with Julian sitting next to me. We talked on the phone every night. We talked about everything.

I blushed. Probably because our recent conversations had been about sex.

Not how me and Gideon talked about sex. Julian wasn't forceful. He was quiet. Respectful. He seemed like he wanted to make me feel good instead of hurting me.

I leaned further into his chest and he rubbed my forehead. I closed my eyes taking in his scent.

We'd talked on the phone about what we might do our first time being together. How it would be. How much he loved me.

Love. It still felt weird to think about the word.

"You sure you ok?" He asked.

"Yeah."

"That's good."

We watched TV for a while. Mom was at church. She wouldn't be home until after nine. It was only 6:30. We watched a tabloid show about which celebrities had gotten plastic surgery and who was dating who. We laughed at the different segments. Julian teased me about actors I liked. The whole time he rubbed my head.

When the show went off he cleared his throat. "Can I kiss you?"

I looked into his eyes. He wasn't talking about the peck on the lips he'd give me at school. He wanted a real kiss.

I nodded.

I parted my lips as he leaned forward. We connected and he slipped his tongue into my mouth gently. His breath smelled like peppermint gum. I gasped as he explored my mouth. He pulled me closer, his hand on my lower back.

The more we kissed the more relaxed I got. His kiss was electrifying. I wasn't afraid of Julian. I didn't think he was going to hurt me. He wasn't forcing himself on me like Gideon used to.

Julian pulled away and cupped my chin. "You know

I love you, right?"

I nodded. "Let's go downstairs."

CHAPTER 5

 Iheld the phone against my ear and huffed as I tried to find something to watch on the television. "What do you like about me?"

"Everything." Julian said.

I flipped through the channels without waiting to see what was on. "'Everything,' is not an answer."

"Yes it is, you're smart, pretty, you got a good head on your shoulders…"

I stopped flipping channels. "You know I hate when people say that.'"

Julian laughed. "I like everything…"

Me and Julian had had this conversation a bunch of times and he always said the same thing. That got on my nerves. How could he like everything about someone? I hadn't told him about me getting kidnapped. He didn't know how jacked up my family was.

"Whatchu like about me?"

"Ummm…" I thought about it.

I liked that I didn't have to try hard. We could be on the phone for hours, sometimes we'd talk a lot. We'd tell each other about our day or watch TV. Sometimes we'd just hold the phone. I didn't have to impress him. Still, I couldn't think of what to say that I "liked" about him. I didn't have to worry about him cheating. He was always there, but that didn't mean I liked him. I liked how he treated me. I didn't want to say that, though.

"I like how sweet you are." I said.

"Aww, man, make sure you don't tell my boys I'm sweet."

"But you *are* sweet…"

Julian took me out a lot; we were always at the mall. His mom would pick me up and drop us off wherever we wanted to go. I went to church with them, too. Julian and I would hold hands in the wooden pews, and their pastor would have me stand up to let the congregation know there was a visitor. We'd have dinner afterwards, and I'd play cards with his little brother while him and his mom kicked it in the kitchen. I was part of their family. Me and Julian would lay in his room talking until his mom took me home at night.

Julian worked at the skating rink on 28th street. He'd pay for me to come up there and check on me during his breaks to make sure I was having fun. He didn't get a lot of hours, but he stacked his money. He paid for everything we did. He hooked me up on my birthday. He brought me clothes, balloons and candy to school; my girls were geeked when they saw all my gifts, but I still didn't know what I "liked" about him.

Liking somebody made me nervous, like I was losing control. I'd been nervous since Julian told me he loved me. I didn't feel lovable.

I wanted to be with him, but I was used to liking whoever liked me. I had never thought about what I liked about a person. I just kicked it with whoever wanted me.

Me and Julian had had sex that day he came over. I was waiting on him to disappear, but he still spent just as much time with me. That was crazy to me.

I changed the subject. "What do you want to be when you grow up?"

"I'mma be a rapper."

"A rapper, Julian?"

"You think that's funny?"

"Yeah!"

"Why is that?

"For one thing, it's not a job —"

"Yes it is."

"No it isn't!" I laughed.

"Don't tell me you doubting me. You already know I got skills."

Julian could flow. He'd rap at breakfast, in the hallways, on the phone at night when I was falling asleep on him. All he did was rap.

"You're good. But you gotta have a backup plan."

"I don't need one, boo."

"Julian…"

"Stop worrying. You gon' be mad when I make it big."

"No I'm not."

"Alright. Let's bet. I'mma make it big, and when I make you rich, don't say nothing."

"You so silly…"

Julian started flowing over a beat he'd been bobbing his head to at school that day.

"Julian." I called his name over his rhymes.

I paused. "Julian."

"*Uh-uh, uh-uh...*" He ad libbed over his beat.

"Julian."

"What, girl?"

"Stop!"

"I don't need no backup plan," He chuckled. "Watch. I'mma blow up and you ain't gonna be laughing."

I shook my head. "Okay."

"What are you gonna be...besides my wife?"

"Shut up, Julian."

"I'm serious," He went back to humming the beat. "One day you are gonna be my wife."

I hesitated. "What makes you so sure?"

"Because, I love you..." He kept on humming.

This wasn't the first time Julian had talked about me being his wife. I liked when he said it. It made me feel good. At the same time it made me start wondering what he liked about me all over again. He didn't know my life.

"I'mma own a business." I said.

We talked about how I wanted to go to Spelman. I

told him he had to go to college, too. I didn't know why I wanted to go to school for business. I knew I'd be good at it, but I really loved people. I wanted to be a social worker. One time I'd told my brother, Garret I wanted to open up a group home for teenage moms. That didn't seem like work to me.

I loved helping people. If someone was sad, or having a bad day, I could always tell. I was drawn to them. I'd talk to kids I barely knew at school if I felt like something was wrong. I liked helping them figure things out. I was starting to think I should be a counselor. Dad wouldn't go for that. Since he was an engineer he pushed me and my brothers to get a professional degree. I was going to major in business to make him happy until I figured out what to do.

Julian interrupted my thoughts, "Let's make a commitment."

"What kind of commitment?"

"To stay together."

"What's that mean?" I asked. "We're still in high school."

"It means we gon' ride for each other. I'm not going nowhere, and you ain't going nowhere."

My hands tensed up and I changed the subject.

"You got any tests tomorrow?"

"Nah, I don't think so…"

I glanced at the answering machine, halfway listening to Julian. A guy I used to kick it with, Teddy had called. I hadn't returned his phone call. I didn't know if I would. I wasn't sure I wanted to deal with him.

Julian and I talked for another hour before his mom picked up the other receiver. "Get off that phone…"

"Alright, ma."

"—Y'all go to the same school."

"Ma, *alright…*"

"— And you act like you ain't gon' see that girl again, don't you got homework? Tell Tiffany you'll see her tomorrow." She put the receiver down.

Julian chuckled. "Gotta go, boo."

"Your mom is a trip."

"Man, I know."

"I love her though, I'll see you in the morning.

"Alright, I get paid Friday. Don't forget to figure out what you wanna do."

CHAPTER 6

"Moms said you should come to Christmas dinner with us." Julian said. "We're going to my Grandmother's."

"Okay." It was already Christmas Eve, but I didn't have plans.

"We'll pick you up in the morning, she said you gotta go to church, too."

I groaned. "Ugh…"

"Come on, don't be like that."

"I don't want to," I whined.

"You know how Moms is."

I didn't have a problem with church, but I wasn't in the mood. I never understood what the pastor was talking about and I didn't like how they made me stand up and say my name every week.

Mom used to try to make me go to church. One time she said I *had* to go or I couldn't live with her anymore. Dad was furious. He said I could come live with him any time. Mom backed down as soon as I said I was leaving.

Something about church reminded me of when I was little and Dad was directing the choir. Everyone was happy then. Maybe it reminded me of what I was missing. Julian's mom was cool, but I wasn't about to be going to church with them all the time.

"I know, I just don't want to." I played with the phone cord.

Mom didn't try to force me to go anymore.

"I'm giving you to God, Tiffany. I'mma let the Lord handle you, I'm at my wits end."

"Whatever."

"Don't be disrespectful."

Mom said she was surrendering me to God. That she wasn't going to try to make me do anything concerning church anymore since she'd tried everything she could. She said she wasn't forcing me to have a relationship because all she was doing was pushing me farther away. All I heard was she was giving up.

I was confused. Mom couldn't say two words to me

without me getting mad. I didn't know why I was so angry. I just was. The sound of her voice felt like chalk being scraped across a blackboard. And she was giving up. I was only a teenager. I didn't understand, she was giving me what I wanted when I wasn't sure of what I wanted.

"The Lord is gonna handle you..."

I sighed loudly into the phone.

"Come on bae, I want you to be there."

"Alright." I leaned my head back into the couch. "I'll see you tomorrow."

***

"What's up Grams," Julian hugged his grandmother as we walked into her bright kitchen.

"Merry Christmas, baby," She reached up to kiss him on the cheek. "I'm glad y'all made it. I was starting to think your mom got lost."

"Hey, Mama," Julians's mother put a bowl of potato salad on the counter and hugged the elderly woman.

"I'm glad we made it too." Julian looked around. "You ain't done with dinner yet?"

"Boy," She shoo'd him with her dishrag. "Go sit

your butt down somewhere."

"I'm just playin'," Julian kissed her temple. "You know I love you, Grams."

I waved "hello" as Julian hugged the rest of his family. We'd just gotten back from church. I'd met most of them already when I'd visited his grandmother's house for Thanksgiving. A few of his cousins went to school with us.

"Come on, bae." Julian took my hand and led me through the kitchen. The food smelled good. The dining room table had ham, greens, macaroni and cheese, and a makeshift table at the end had just desserts on it.

The setup reminded me of my cousin Tracy's Thanksgiving dinners in Detroit. I followed Julian into the living room and his little brother pat the space next to him on the couch. "You wanna sit by me?"

I smiled. "Sure."

Julian punched Tyrell playfully in the chest. "You always tryna' get with my girl, little punk."

Tyrell laughed. "Stop!"

"What I tell you about hittin' on my woman?"

Tyrell blocked Julian's punches. "You just mad. She likes me better than you, anyways."

I faked a gasp. "Ooohhh, Tyrell!"

"What?" Julian put him in a headlock and roughed up his hair.

"Stop, Julian!" Tyrell doubled over laughing, letting out a high pitched shriek.

"You gon' let him talk to me like that, boo?"

"He might be right," I teased.

"Now you got my girl, siding with you…" Julian took another jab.

"Leave my friend alone." I plopped down next to Tyrell, putting my arm around his shoulder to protect him as he grinned up at his brother.

"You lucky, chump." Julian pointed two fingers at Tyrell, squinting his eyes.

Tyrell stuck his tongue out.

"That's it," Julian tickled us and we fell sideways into the deep cushions of the sofa.

"Both of y'all need to stop!" I laughed.

We kicked it in the living room while the little kids played video games until Julian's grandmother told us it was time to come eat.

"Jermaine?" She called his older cousin.

"One sec, Granny." He tapped his controller, twisting it to the side.

"Come on in here and say grace. The food is already getting cold..."

"Y'all come on." Jermaine set his controller down and got up off the couch.

Julian's family filed into the kitchen. When everyone got there we held hands in a circle.

"Y'all quiet down," Jermaine cleared his throat as Julian's aunt cut her eyes at the kids. "*Dear God, thank you for this day. Thank you for allowing us to celebrate Christmas with our family, and thank you for allowing us to see another year with our loved ones. Most importantly, thank you for sending Jesus...*"

Julian's Granny beamed over the top of his head at Jermaine. "Amen," she said loudly when he finished his prayer. She opened the oven and pulled out a pan of sweet potatoes and put them on the table, looking satisfied. "Let the little kids get their plates."

The sweet potatoes smelled like dessert. Steam seeped from a thick layer of marshmallows that were baked over the top of the dish.

My mouth watered. I was hungry after sitting in church all morning.

Granny pursed her lips. She looked at me out the corner of her eye as she wiped down the cabinets. I clasped my hands in front of me. I'd been to her house a couple times but I'd never felt welcome. She made me uncomfortable.

Granny shuffled to the stove and got another pan. She caught my eye. "Baby, don't your family want to be with you on Christmas?"

"Mama..." Julian's mother shook her head.

"What?" Granny shot an irritated look at her.

"Mama," Aunt Gail widened her eyes.

"Well, I'm just asking." Granny said. Her lip quivered.

Jermaine put his fist over his mouth to cover his laugh.

"Dang Grams..." Julian shook his head.

My chest tightened as I tried to come up with an answer that sounded right. Why *was* I there? My brothers hardly ever came home. Garret and Nigel worked out of town and Rodney was away at college. They'd go to their friends houses for holidays. They tried their hardest to stay away. Probably because it made them sad to be there, like it made me. Mom was at church, and Dad wouldn't be visiting for a couple months. Nobody was missing me. "We spend holidays together," I stuttered, "but ... I'll see them later."

"Hmph," Granny went back to setting out food. "Seems strange if you ask me."

"Granny..." Jermaine laughed with a "you know how Granny is" look.

I stood in line to get my food behind Julian's cousins. I couldn't believe what his grandmother had said. She was mean. I didn't want to be there anymore. I unclenched my hands, trying to keep calm.

Julian put his hand on my shoulder. He whispered. "You know my granny don't like you, right?"

"Why?" I snapped my head as I turned towards him.

"Shhh..." He whispered. He handed me a plate.

"Why not?"

"She says you're 'fast'."

My heart sped up. "What are you talking about?" I stopped scooping green beans onto my plate. "What did I ever do 'fast' in front of your granny?"

"Calm down," He said, cracking up.

"It's not funny!" I let the spoon drop and punched

him in the arm.

"Ahhh, quite playing!"

I felt my cheeks getting hot. "What I do to your granny?" I whispered.

"She says she can just tell, boo." Julian poured me a cup of punch and smirked. "I told her you ain't 'fast' around nobody but me."

"Don't say stuff like that," I punched him again. "Your granny is mean."

"Shhh," He put his finger to his lips and grabbed my hand. "Be quiet before she hears you."

"Don't nobody care…" I pouted.

Julian took my plate and carried it into the living room. "Don't be sad baby," he grinned, "You know my mom likes you.

"Still…"

I took my plate back as I sat on the couch, thinking about his grandmother's comments. I thought about how she would look at me when the pastor asked if anyone wanted to be saved at the end of church. I never stood up for that. One time she'd asked what church I attended and I told her I didn't really go much.

"Any girl in my grandson's life needs to have a

relationship with Jesus..."

What did she know about my "relationship" with Jesus? I believed there was a God, but the prayer I prayed that night with Mom's friends probably didn't qualify me as being saved. Not anymore. I didn't do what saved people did, and I didn't want to. I didn't even understand what being "saved" meant. Saved from what? Julian's grandmother sounded like my mom. Judgemental. I'd said the prayer and tried to change, but if God wanted to save me, he should have saved me from all the stuff I'd already gone through. He should have saved me from Gideon.

I thought about the way people at Julian's church looked at me. Were they thinking the same thing as his grandmother? Did she know more than Julian did? How could she call me 'fast' when she didn't even know me?

I didn't appreciate Julian laughing, like it was a joke.

Saved.

His granny could keep her "saved," I wouldn't come around her or her church again.

"Don't worry, boo," Julian bit into his food, still laughing, "I know all about you, and I love you."

"Whatever..."

CHAPTER 7

"What's up baby?"

"Hey," I opened the front door wide and Jeff leaned in to kiss my temple. His breath smelled like menthol. Probably from smoking Newports. I stood on my toes and winter air wrapped around his warm hug.

"Lemme get my keys." I looked around the living room to make sure I wasn't forgetting anything.

"Alright." Jeff made himself comfortable. He'd been over a couple times. I took a breath and pushed thoughts of Julain down. What he didn't know wouldn't hurt him.

I grabbed my keys off the end table and turned the television off as Jeff ran his hand across one of Mom's African figurines. "You have a good day at school today?"

"Yeah…"

He turned toward me. "That's good, what you do?"

"Same ol' stuff."

"Like?"

I told him about the project I'd done in science class.

"That's good, baby girl."

Jeff was already out of school. He was 23.

He grabbed my belt loop and the hairs stood up on the back of my neck. "You ready?" He pulled me towards himself.

I tucked my hair behind my ear and glanced at the kitchen clock. "Yeah." I gave him a weak smile. It was only 7:00, so I had time.

I glanced at the door. I shouldn't have left it open. I didn't want any neighbors telling Mom I had a guy over. Miss Sheba from four doors down and Mom had gotten cool. They would stand outside and talk about church for hours when Mom got out of work. Church. Miss Sheba made sure she talked to everybody on our side of the complex. She knew everyone's business and would act like she didn't realize she was gossiping when she told you something you didn't know. She'd wave at me like we were cool, but she'd started watching who I had in and out.

"*Damn*, you smell good." Jeff's breath tickled my ear. His hands cupped my hips as he pulled me closer.

"Just a sec…" I slid from his grasp and ran upstairs. I grabbed my purse off my dresser and turned off the light.

Mom was at church and Julian was at work at the skating rink. It was Friday night so he'd be there at least till 11:30.

I ran back down the steps. "I'm ready."

"Cool," Jeff caught me up and kissed me. "Come here." He slid his hands down my waist and unlatched my belt.

"Wait," I lurched forward, swallowing hard. I pushed my hands against his chest as a reflex.

I shouldn't do this…

Jeff was something like my boyfriend. He'd asked me to be his girlfriend a couple weeks earlier even though we hardly knew each other, and I'd said yes. I didn't know much about him except that he was cute and his cousin was a famous boxer. He'd talk to me about boxing matches and pay per view fights I'd never seen. He didn't know about Julian.

He whispered. "You fine as hell, wait for what?"

"Jeff," I giggled, pulling away. I wiped my lips free of saliva and I glanced at the open door.

"I'm for real." He cupped my face and pulled my lip into his mouth, kissing me.

I looked down. "Thanks." I re-buckled my belt and wiped my palms. I didn't realize they'd gotten so sweaty. I ran my hands across my jeans and flexed my fingers outward. "Ready?" I asked. Cold air whipped around me, cooling me off.

"Let's go." He slapped my butt, eyeing my hips.

I kept my head down as I walked to Jeff's car. I didn't want one of Julian's friends to see me. I felt guilty. I had talked to Julian right before he went to work. I slid into the passenger's seat and scooched down.

I glanced at Jeff as he put his keys in the ignition. His slender frame was just muscular enough to tell he was a grown man. His slanted eyes were tight. His jaw had sharp angles and his skin was like teakwood.

The tension in my chest eased as he pulled onto Charring Cross and made a left onto Rowland Drive.

Jeff was a dope boy. He'd pick me up and take me with him when he sold rocks to the coke heads in the city. Sometimes we'd stop at the corner store to get chicken and fries with hot sauce and garlic pepper, but mostly we just rode around.

Rain slapped the windshield as we rode. We didn't

talk much. Wutang blasted through his stereo system.

Minutes passed before Jeff came to a stop and threw his head up at me. "Come in." He opened the car door and stepped out, pulling his Polo jacket close to his chest.

I looked out the window, surprised. Slush mixed with rain and ice made it hard to see. He'd pulled up to a big fourplex with a wraparound porch. The lawn looked like it hadn't been cut that year and trash littered the ground, clogging the drain pipes.

I usually waited in the car when Jeff dropped off his packages.

I got out and followed him up the steps. I could smell the inside of the downstairs apartment before we got on the porch. It smelled like used cooking grease.

We got inside and a skinny lady with a crooked smile came out the back. "Hey Jeff, baby! You alright?" Her voice sounded like it hurt to talk. Like gravel. I wanted to cover my nose. I couldn't tell where the smell was coming from. The living room was clean, but filth seemed like it was coming out the house's pores.

"I'm cool." Jeff gave the lady a side hug.

"Where you been at?"

"I been around," He nodded towards the sofa.

"Have a seat."

"Y'all alright?" She asked again.

"We good." Jeff threw his head up. He unzipped his coat pocket and looked inside. He zipped it again impatiently.

The lady plopped a baby down next to me on the couch. "Could you watch her for a second?"

The woman's biker shorts looked like the ones I used to wear in 4th grade with my white Minnie Mouse sweatshirt. She was skin and bones. Her elbows and knees jut out of her clothes like branches, like they would snap if the wind blew too hard. The lady's shorts had stains on them and a safety pin on one side, keeping them together . She had a kind smile even though one of her teeth was missing.

"Sure."

"I'll be right back." She followed Jeff into the back room.

I smiled at the baby and held my finger out for her to grab. She had dust colored skin and plaits in her hair that stuck up all over her head. Black and orange and pink and green and red barrettes made her hair look like a messy rainbow. Her eyes were set far apart like an alien. She looked around two. I tried to play with her but she stared at me like she was in a coma. She didn't smile.

I leaned back into the couch. The cushions felt like weathered corduroy against my fingers. I folded my hands in my lap and focused on the TV. VH1 was on. The top 10 music video countdown. I wished we could afford cable. I was always missing out, but I would never ask for it. Most of my friends had Comcast, but Mom didn't have money for extras.

I glanced at the little girl. I wondered if I should change the channel to something like Sesame Street.

I looked around the living room for a remote.

"Let's go baby," Jeff came out the bedroom and motioned for me to get up.

"Where?" I stood, making sure the baby didn't fall.

"Alright nah, see you later Jeff, baby!" The lady said, her voice too loud for us all to be inside.

He held the door open. "I gotta make another run."

"What was wrong with the baby?" I asked once we were back in the car.

"Whatchu mean?"

I shrugged. "She didn't move. She just stared."

Jeff put his arm over my seat and looked behind him as he switched lanes. "She's a crack baby."

My throat went dry as he bent the corner.

"Stay here," He pulled up to another house and snatched the keys out the ignition.

"Okay…" Crack baby. I imagined the little girl staring into space. Her dusty pale skin, she looked like she'd never played outside in the sun.

Jeff held his pants up with his pockets as he ran up the sidewalk. He was in the house by the time a tear slid down my cheek.

I focused my gaze outside. Rain trickled down a sliver of ice that was forming on the windshield. When Jeff got done he would probably take me to his Dad's house. We'd hung out there earlier in the week. It was the first time we'd had sex.

Guilt pierced my heart. Julian went on break in a couple hours. I wanted to talk to him. If I was back by 10, I'd be there when he called.

CHAPTER 8

"Heyyy, that's my song," Tori turned the radio up, snapping her fingers. "Come on y'all, we playin'?"

"Yeah," I said. "Let's play."

We were in Tori's basement. Her mom's oriental rug did a good job at blocking out the cold from the cement floor. I propped my oversized pillow up and danced to the music coming through her stereo system.

"Heyyy, heyyy...heyyy, heyyy..." Tori took a drink out the glass she was holding and shuffled a deck of cards. It was Saturday night and her mom was asleep upstairs. We were waiting on Shae to get back from dropping off her little brother.

"—Like I was saying," Shonda said, cracking up, "I can't *believe* you don't be getting caught, Tiffany."

"*What* Shonda?" I hid behind my glass.

"You know *what*." She mocked my voice.

"Shonda, quit laughing at me!"

"Whatever sister." She picked up the cards Tori had dealt. "I don't even know why I'm surprised."

"Shonda…"

"I already know how you are."

"Shondaaa."

"Uh-uh," She cut her eyes. "Don't '*Shonda*' me. Tiffany, you know you wrong."

I held up my drink. "I'm not cheating."

"What-ever."

"I'm *not*…" I picked my cards up and crossed my legs.

"You need to slow your butt down before it backfires on you."

"I'm being good."

Shonda stared at me with a deadpan look.

I poked my lip out and we all burst out laughing.

"Stop, Shonda." I whined. "I tried!"

"Whatever," She picked through her cards,

organizing her hand, "I don't wanna hear it." She absentmindedly looked through her deck. "You couldn't be faithful if you wanted to."

Shonda and Tori had met at Ottawa. She lived behind Camelot in the apartments by the duck pond. Her and I became friends when I had learned how to take the bus from Mom's to stay the night with Tori.

"Dang," Tori dealt the cards, still laughing. "Shonda, you crazy."

"You *know* I'mma tell the truth."

"You right..." Tori looked at me with raised eyebrows.

"She's *not* right!" I threw my pillow.

"Yes she is, sister," Tori dealt the last few cards. "We all know how Shonda is..."

"—Mean!" I interrupted.

Tori tilted her head, sympathetically. "But you know you could slow down."

Shonda glanced at me over her cards. "Who all you messing with?" She held her fingers up, "three, four other dudes besides Julian?"

I almost spit my drink on the basement floor, "Shonda, you *stupid!*" I pushed her hand aside.

Tori hollered, "Shonda, you foul."

"What? It's hard to keep track!"

Me and Julian had been together for some months. At first I had stopped messing with other dudes. I was happy being with just him. I liked the attention he gave me and how we were always together, but after a while I didn't feel right. What his granny had said about me being fast had pissed me off. I was nice around Julian's family. I didn't appreciate how she acted like she knew me.

Shonda mouthed the words to the song while she sorted her hand. "I don't know who you think you're fooling, girl..."

I put my head down like I was concentrating on my cards.

That day at Christmas dinner had been overwhelming. It felt like Julian's granny could see through me. How did she know? I had never told anyone how I felt. If I wasn't getting attention from more than one person I felt empty inside.

I'd been kicking it with other guys since a couple weeks after me and Julian decided to be together.

I had stopped talking to Jeff. Seeing the little girl at the lady's house made me sad. I couldn't believe she was born addicted to drugs. How could he not care? After that day I didn't want to be around him. Plus, I felt guilty cheating on Julian.

Just not enough to stop.

Shonda shot me a look that was similar to the one Julian's granny had given me a few weeks earlier.

Between Tori, Shonda, Brianne, and Shae, Shonda was our blunt friend. She was always mad about something that had to do with me and Tori.

Shonda shook her head. "Julian don't know what he got himself into."

Tori's friends loved me, especially Shonda. She had a soft spot for me, even though she acted like I got on her nerves. We all said she was mean. She was quick to tell you about yourself and have you feeling stupid. She couldn't stand how crazy I was about boys, or how much Tori drank. Shonda didn't drink or smoke. Sometimes when we made her mad, talking about what we were doing she would get up and go home. We'd be crackin' up, like, *"Where you going, Shonda?"*

She wouldn't say anything. She'd just leave. One time we called and begged her to come back.

"I'm tired of chillin' with y'all... y'all some hoes."

We died laughing.

"Shonda!"

"Uh-uh, I ain't finna keep dealing with y'all and all these dudes, y'all trifling."

It would take a few days, but she'd always come back.

Tori danced in her seat. "I like Julian, Tiff, y'all are cute together."

I laid down my card. "I like him too."

"Oh my God," Shonda rolled her eyes.

"Stop." I threw my hand at her, "I didn't cheat for a long time, Shonda."

"Haaa!" She pushed Tori, "This girl is crazy!"

Tori shook her head, smiling like we had an inside joke.

I studied my hand, trying not to feel guilty.

I didn't want to feel anything.

Tori's basement was calm that weekend; we usually had guys lined up to chill. Tori kicked it with a couple dope boys she had met in school. They'd buy us food and drinks, and we'd hang in the basement or go riding around. Whenever they came, they'd bring a friend for me. Most of the guys Tori knew were grown and out of high school. I was taller than my friends, so I could pass for older.

Guys couldn't believe my age. Their eyes would get big like, *"You can't be in the 10th grade..."*

We always told them how old I was; me and Tori got a kick out of it. They'd act like they didn't want to chill with me, but when it came down to it they always did.

Since Camelot was walking distance from the mall we'd be there every Saturday to see who would try to get with us. We had a bunch of guy friends. My life revolved around who we were talking to.

Tori was kicking it with this guy named Trey. He had a friend named Blaque who had the prettiest dimples. They would come by and we'd cook and have card parties. Me and Blaque had the type of relationship where we never messed around, but we loved each other. We stayed in each other's face. Whenever we were together, he treated me like I was his. He was the type of dude that I would get mad at, if he ever got a girl.

Then there was Teddy. I had met him over the summer when I was walking home. Him and his cousin had pulled up next to me and Teddy rolled down his window so he could talk.

Me and Teddy had messed around before school

started. He was from Detroit, so I didn't have to worry about seeing him as much. It was hard trying to balance Julian and my other friends. It was easier for me to put some distance between me and Teddy because he'd disappear for long periods of time.

"Both of y'all, crazy." Shonda shook her head.

Tori held her hands up. "Don't bring me into this."

"Y'all act just alike."

Shonda didn't deal with guys like me and Tori, so I didn't tell her everything. She didn't know about Jeff. Sometimes I didn't even tell Tori about all the guys I was talking to.

I knew Tori felt responsible for me because she was older, like it was her fault I was acting crazy. She thought she could take more than me without getting hurt.

Shonda was still mad at us from the week before when we went to Tori's friend, Rick's, apartment.

We'd kicked it with Rick a couple times. I thought back to the weekend he had invited us to his frat house. I was scared walking up his rickety wooden steps.

There were some guys that were older than Tori in the doorways, hanging off each other, talking loud and yelling over the music that echoed through the three story house.

I had wrinkled up my nose. It smelled like the inside of a locker room. Me and Tori stepped over beer cans as Rick led us down a hallway of small bedrooms that looked like they had never been cleaned. *"You can sit in here, ain't nobody gon' bite,"* Rick yelled over the music. I sat on his frat brother's beds while him and Tori shared a 40.

By the time Rick had invited us to his crib I was comfortable with him. He looked out. Whenever he came by Tori's he brought me food, and he didn't expect me to drink. He was one of the only guys that treated me like my age.

When we got to Rick's apartment I realized his roommate was this guy named Mike that I liked. He was tall and had a bald head. I'd had a crush on him ever since I saw him working at Foot Locker. I would walk by his store to see if he'd notice me.

I pinched Tori when I realized who Mike was and she gave me an excited look.

We kicked it in the living room, Rick gave me a wine cooler out the refrigerator while him and Tori did shots, then he pulled out a deck of cards.

I was geeked when Mike finally spoke.

"What's up, babygirl?" He threw his head up from the opposite side of the room.

Tori and Rick were cracking jokes while Rick dealt us our hand, but Mike didn't say too much. He was polite, but he stayed in his chair at the dining room table.

"How old are you?" He collected his cards.

I told him and his face darkened.

"You sure?" He rubbed his temples. *"You don't look like no high schooler."* He turned to Rick. *"You got me chillin' it with a 10th grader?"*

"She's cool people." Rick threw a card.

Tori waved her drink. *"You know you like my girl."*

We finished a game of spades and Rick and Tori went to hang out in his room. I put my feet up on the couch and listened to music. After a while, Mike came to sit by me.

I was excited. I thought he was going to try to have sex. I was down. Especially since I'd liked him for a couple years. I pushed thoughts of Julian out of my mind. What he didn't know wouldn't hurt him. Mike asked me about school and if I played any sports.

"Oh, yeah?" He responded after each question like he wasn't paying attention. He put his arm over my shoulder, pulled it away, then got up and stretched. When he sat back down he was farther away. After we

kicked it for a while he went into the bedroom to ask Rick when we were leaving since he was the one driving me and Tori home.

When he came back he laid on the couch across from me, covered his face with his hands and breathed out a loud sigh. A few minutes passed, then he rolled over and went to sleep.

Pshh, he must have a girl.

I went to sleep irritated. We didn't make it home until the following day.

Shonda thought I was a mess. She didn't understand why I did the things I did. I'd been dealing with a bunch of different guys ever since Gideon, and when I finally decided to slow down, I got with Julian. I'd tried to change, but I didn't know how. Shonda didn't understand that.

I didn't either.

I didn't feel right with just one person. Shonda would get mad when Tori would tell her what we had gotten into.

"...I ain't finna be messing with either of y'all hoes in a minute."

Me and Tori would be cracking up, and Shonda would be looking at us with a straight face. She didn't care. She wouldn't even laugh when she said it. We were all so cool that even if we didn't say anything, we could look at each other and tell what the other one was thinking.

We told each other almost everything, and Shonda thought I was a ho.

"Seriously, though?" Shonda threw down a card. "Ain't nobody ever gonna tame you, Tiff. I love that about you."

"I'm for real Shonda, this time I'mma be good."

"Yeah right…"

Tori shook her head. "You gotta slow down, sister…"

Tori didn't care what people thought about her. That's what made being around her so much fun. She didn't care if anyone laughed at her jokes, or if we got invited to parties, and we always did. She said the first thing that came to her mind and people loved her. She didn't care if she ended up dating any of the guys we talked to. She was fine with just having friends.

My feelings would be all involved and she'd be on to the next guy. Her and Shonda thought I was crazy — crying because someone I was cheating with did me wrong. I liked how Tori could have so much fun and not get attached. I was always upset about one of my "boyfriends". I was the one cheating on Julian, but I didn't want the guys I messed with to stop wanting me.

Shonda swayed to the music, "Tiff, you ain't gon' know how to act when this backfires."

"Shondaaa…" I groaned.

I didn't know what my problem was. Julian loved me. Everything was perfect, but I couldn't stand it.

"You are mean." I said, giggling.

"No I'm not, I'm honest."

I thought back to the previous school year. Gideon had disappeared and I'd felt like Dad had abandoned me. I'd needed someone to fill the hole in my heart they'd left. After messing with Gideon I'd decided no one was going to take advantage of me. If I was going to have sex, it was going to be because I wanted to. I was worse than Hannah — sleeping with everybody. It made me feel like I'd regained control.

Julian's granny was right. Days before I'd gone to her house for Christmas, Teddy had called to say he was in town.

"What's up, Tiff?"

"Nothing."

"I've missed you. You should hang out with me."

"Teddy, I told you I got a boyfriend the last time you were here."

"Dang, girl. We ain't gon' do nothing. It's Dwight's birthday. I was just calling to let you know about the party."

Teddy's cousin, Dwight lived down the street off Camelot Drive.

I hesitated. *"He's having a party?"*

"Yeah, I'm throwing it for him. He turns 21 next week."

"Hmph…"

"Come on, Tiff. It's not like it's going to just be me and you. It's a party…"

Teddy picked me up that night in an all white Cadillac and took me to the Crowne Plaza on 28th street.

"Teddy…" My mouth fell open when he used his key card to open the hotel room door. The room was beautiful. It was an open suite with a king-sized bed.

I turned on my heels. *"Where is everybody?"*

"They coming…"

"Teddy, you're a liar."

"No I'm not." He caught me by the arm. *"I told you*

they coming. I thought we could just kick it alone before they got here."

"Let go of me."

Teddy dropped my arm. *"Tiff..."*

"Take me back."

"Come on, just hang out with me…"

"No!"

I stayed for an hour, then Teddy took me home. I was mad at him for lying and saying there was a party, but I was used to having sex with dudes I was mad at. Like Jeff. Something inside of me wouldn't let me say "no" and mean it.

A couple days later Julian's granny was asking me why my family didn't want to spend Christmas with me.

My granny thinks you're fast…

Tori held up the bottle of liquor we'd been drinking from. "You want the last of this?"

"Yeah." I handed my glass to her.

"Lush…" Shonda mumbled.

"Oooohhh, Shonda," Tori said. "Just because you don't drink—"

"I'm just playing with y'all."

I laughed, thinking about what Shonda had said.

Ain't nobody gonna tame you...

"Go 'head." Tori nodded at the stack of cards on the floor. "Your turn."

I took a sip of my drink and looked intently at my hand. I didn't know what was wrong with me. My heart felt like it had been shattered. Like if I tried to pick up the pieces, I wouldn't know where they fit. If I tried to fix myself I'd get cut. I wanted somebody to tame me. I wanted somebody to love me so much that I'd stop acting crazy.

CHAPTER 9

"*H*eyyy, girl…" Kendra took her seat next to me and scooched in. I was hoping she wouldn't miss our bus.

"What's up, girl?" I slid over to give her more room. She threw her backpack under the seat in front of us and moved around to find a good position to close her eyes. "*Girl*, I am so done after the weekend we had."

"Me too." I scooched close to the window and leaned on the glass. I still felt tipsy from Saturday.

Kendra smoothed her hair around her neck, making sure she didn't mess her wrap up and leaned against the seat. The piney scent of the seat's cracked leather overwhelmed my nose. I let my mind drift. We wouldn't be sleeping during the ride to school; Monday mornings got hype.

"Hey you two," Cole sat behind us. "What y'all get

into this time?" He looked us over with mock concern. "Looks like you made it out okay."

"What-ever Cole," Kendra reached over the seat and punched him.

"Cut it out, that's my bad arm!" Cole teased. "I'm just making sure y'all made it back to reality."

"You don't gotta worry 'bout us," Kendra smoothed her jet black hair around her head. "We got everything under control."

Mom loved Kendra's hair. She commented on how healthy her bob looked every time Kendra stopped by. *"That girl must go to the shop once a week..."* She'd say it reminded her of her grandmother's Native American roots.

Cole gave us a look, like, "yeah right," and opened a book.

The bus took off with a *whoosh* and seconds later pulled up to a stop a few blocks down East Paris.

Dang, these stops are close, I thought. I still had a hangover from Saturday and only got three hours of sleep on Sunday night. The bus ride was making me sick.

"I can't wait until next weekend," Kendra said, "We gotta plan what we're gon' do..."

It was halfway through the semester, and Kendra and I had been hanging out since a couple weeks after school started. Her mom was kinda like mine — easygoing — plus Kendra was a year older than me and the rest of our friends, so she could do what she wanted without getting in trouble.

"My boy can get us drinks," Kendra said, "We just gotta give him the money…"

Me and Kendra had gotten cool when she moved into the apartments where Shonda lived, behind Camelot. Kendra was popular. Everywhere we went people knew her, or knew of her from school. She had two best friends, Amber and Morgan. Amber had already graduated. We'd all get together and chill with me and Tori's friends. We got along well.

I repositioned myself and closed my eyes.

It was weird how I had gotten used to having two sets of friends.

My friends that I had grown up with since elementary school were different from me and Tori's friends. Their parents asked where they were going. They couldn't stay out all night or come and go as they pleased. I couldn't tell my school friends everything I was getting into, but now I had Kendra.

***

"Hey Tiff, hey Kendra!" Nicole and Ashley perked up when they got on the bus and saw us sitting in the back.

"Hey ya'll," I waved at the line of tired kids filing onto our bus. I could relate to the distant "I wish I was still 'sleep," look on their faces.

A girl with a huge smile like sunshine stepped on last. "Who's that?" I tugged on Kendra's sleeve and she turned from talking to Cole.

"Oh my gosh, hey you two!" The new girl beamed as she leaned over the seats to hug Nicole and Ashley. "How have you guys been?" She had honey brown hair with golden blonde weaved through the strands and curls that bounced as she moved. The way her curls framed her face made her smile look bigger than it was.

"Hey, you're back!" Ashley squeezed the girl tight.

"Long time no see!" Ashley's twin, Nicole, got up to hug her.

"I missed y'all!" The girl's smile radiated through the bus. She stood in the aisle greeting everybody that recognized her.

Kendra leaned close enough to whisper. "*Girl*, that's Corrine, she's a ho."

I frowned, "Whatchu you mean, 'she's a ho?' " I wanted to pull my arm away.

Kendra leaned closer, "Girl, she messed with everybody." She lowered her voice. "Even Cole."

I looked at Kendra like she was crazy. Cole didn't get down like that. He was good. If he wasn't reading his Bible he was giving advice.

"I forgot you didn't go to middle school with us." Kendra leaned back into her seat. "She messed with Greg, Koran…"

I stopped listening. I was watching the girl walk towards us. She looked happy.

"Agghhhhh," Corrine screamed when she reached our seat, "Oh my gosh, Kendra!" She bent down. "I haven't seen you in forever!" She rocked Kendra back and forth, hugging her.

"I know girl, I missed you," Kendra leaned in like she was getting choked by Corrine's tight hug. "Where you been?"

I could make out the beachy scent of Corrine's shampoo from where I sat. She must have washed her hair that morning.

"My mom got a job in Detroit," Corrine straightened, smoothing her fly aways down. "So we had to move. But

I'm back!" She bounced on her toes, hair flopping all over. "I'm so happy to see you, do you live out here?"

"Yup," Kendra nodded. "Across the street."

"Agghhhhh!" Corrine screamed. "Me too! We just moved in. We're gonna have so much fun, now!"

"Corrine you crazy…" Kendra shook her head. "Oh yeah," she motioned towards me. "This is my girl Tiff, did ya'll ever meet?

"Hey Tiff!" Corrine smiled, "Uh-uh."

"You must have moved when we were still in the 9th grade building, there's no way Tiffany could have missed your crazy butt."

Corrine threw her floral backpack on the seat next to us and sat. "Well, now you guys will be seeing me all the time."

Kendra nudged my leg under the seat. I wondered what that meant.

"Hi Cole!" Corrine noticed him sitting behind us.

"Hey," Cole smiled wide, "Glad to see you back."

"Thanks…"

Corrine talked with our friends who had filled up the seats around us. I was trying to figure her out when

Kendra grabbed my arm and leaned in close. "So like I was saying, girl. She a mess, she's been with everyone…"

Kendra's words stung. Hearing her describe Corrine made me feel like I was looking in a mirror.

***

"So we were at this club in Flint," Kendra turned to talk to our friends. "Everybody's tryna holla at us—It's like 3 o'clock in the morning, I'm so drunk I can't even dance…"

Corrine crossed one leg underneath herself and rested her chin in her palm.

"Then we meet these guys —" I said.

"They was *fine*. Next thing you know they were asking if we wanted to go to breakfast — it was like, 5 o'clock in the morning!"

"Right!" I added.

"That's what I like about dudes from Flint," Kendra slapped the seat. "They're down to spend money. You can't even get one of these dudes around here to take you on a date." She rolled her eyes at the guys sitting close by and we bust out laughing.

"Hey, hey…" Cole looked up from his book.

"Oh my gosh," Nicole whined, "Y'all *always* having fun. You gotta invite us next time." She looked at her twin.

"Girl," Kenrdra pursed her lips. "I can't wait to go back."

I sat back in my seat and listened to Kendra talk.

I was exhausted.

Kendra's sister, April, had picked me, her and Morgan up that Friday. Kendra had been talking about kicking it with her older sister since I'd met her. Her and Morgan had all kinds of stories about having fun in Flint. That's where Kendra was from. All we had to do was give April gas money.

"Hey Mom." I put my book bag down in the hallway that Tuesday before we left, after school.

"Hey, how was school today?" Mom said from the kitchen.

I went in and gave her a hug. *"It was fine."*

"Good." She went back to cutting potatoes and listening to the news that was on in the living room.

"Mom, can I go out of town with Kendra? Her sister wants us to come to Flint."

"Flint?" Mom's forehead wrinkled.

"Yeah, it's just gonna be us girls."

"What's going on in Flint?" She frowned.

"Kendra's sister just wants to spend time with her. She said we could come."

"Hmm, I don't know about that…"

We got our plan together — I told Mom Kendra's sister was picking her up for the weekend and was letting her bring friends, and Kendra's mom was used to her going out of town. Mom gave in and said I could go as long as there was supervision. The couple times she'd met Kendra, she'd gotten a good impression. I wasn't sure why.

I was excited when Friday came. Kendra had said April would take us to the club and that she'd let us drink.

I didn't know what I expected April to be like, but I thought she would act how my brothers acted. Grown. She was 25. I was thinking we would hang out and do something laid back, I couldn't see a 25-year-old taking some teenagers to the club.

April picked us up after school and we jumped on the highway. She was short and fair-skinned. Nigel would've said she was thick. She was pretty in the opposite way Kendra was. April's car smelled like the cherry air freshener hanging from her mirror mixed with the faint smell of weed.

She was nothing like my brothers. Every couple words she said were cuss words. She had the music turned up, talking about how much fun we were gonna have, hyping us up. Yelling at traffic. Screaming the words to the songs on the radio.

Her and Kendra were more like friends than sisters.

We got to April's house late Friday night and as soon as we put our bags down we started drinking. I didn't realize she was married until I heard her cussing her husband out in her bedroom.

They went back and forth, then they made their way to the living room, screaming at the top of their lungs. April's husband looked like he was about to snap. Instead, he snatched open the front door and slammed it behind him. Kendra closed her eyes like she was exhausted. "Girl, they always like this."

"Right." Morgan laughed. She had been to Flint with Kendra a bunch of times.

"Psshh ... don't nobody care about him *slamming* doors," April danced her way into the kitchen and poured herself a drink. "He can be mad all he wants. Get on my nerves..." April held the bottle out to me. "You want some, pretty girl?" She had been calling me "pretty girl" since Kendra told her my name.

"Uh-uh, this girl is beautiful. I'm calling her 'pretty girl'..."

"No thanks." I didn't know what to expect April to be like, but I didn't expect her to let us get drunk like some adults. My brothers wouldn't have done that.

"Stop...!"

"No, you stop!"

I woke up the next morning to April's sons yelling. She had four boys.

"Quit pushing me 'fore I beat you down!"

I tried to block them out by putting a pillow over my head. I was in the bottom bunk in their room. April had let us take over their bedroom, but her apartment was small, so there was nowhere else for them to play.

"Pshew, pshew, pshew," Kendra's youngest nephew shot a toy gun in my direction and jumped on the ladder.

"Boy, get down!" Kendra threw a pillow and her nephew scrambled across the top bunk. *"Leave, before I tell your mama!"*

I wished she would tell, they were getting on my nerves.

"Pshew, pshew, pshew!"

Me, Kendra and Morgan slept most of the day, then we got up and visited some of Kendra's friends. April was still fussing when we left the house so we wasted time by going to get food. The plan was to go to the club that night. I had never been inside a club. Me and Tori would go to the club and sit outside with guys she was talking to. We'd park and drink in the lot until everyone came outside. I had never thought about going in. I knew I was too young.

When we made it back to the apartment after visiting Kendra's friends April was in a better mood than she was when we left. We laid around, talking, April turned her stereo up and cooked for the boys. "Yall want some chicken?" She fried wing dings with no sides and cracked open another bottle. Her husband came out the back room and April bumped him.

"You play too much." He hugged her and grabbed a wing.

She put ice in a glass and poured him a shot of dark liquor. *"Hey!"* The song changed and she spun with the greasy spatula still in her hand and turned the stereo up. "Monica can *sing!*" She rocked her hips, dancing on her husband while he smiled down at her like she was crazy.

Kendra rolled her eyes. "See…"

We got in the shower later that night. I looked at the clock while I did my makeup. It was getting late. 12:30 rolled around and April still hadn't gotten dressed. I was cool if she didn't want to go to the club anymore. I had started feeling uncomfortable earlier in the day. I didn't know why. I was used to hanging out. I felt like a heavy weight was on my chest. Like I never should have come to Flint.

April came out of her room. "Which shoes you like, pretty girl?" She held up two different pairs of heels.

I looked at the clock. "Where we going?" I thought she had decided not to go.

"Girl, to the after hours." She waved the heels. "That's when the club is *really* poppin'."

***

I cracked my window in April's back seat and watched the city pass by. We turned right onto a deserted street that looked like it would have been busy had it been in a different city. There were busted out windows and burned down storefronts on every other block. We rode past some raggedy houses. Lights shone up ahead of us. It reminded me of a movie scene.

Wet newspaper and Burger King wrappers blocked the rain grates that ran along the sides of the streets.

April turned into a dirt patch that looked like it used to be someone's front yard. I sat up. She accelerated slowly.

"It's about to be hype." April fought to park in the middle of the excitement lit up by her high beams.

"*Aye...aye girl...*" A group of guys stood in the gravel holding red plastic cups. "*Aye, lemme holla at you...*"

Girls positioned themselves in between the cars wearing dresses and heels, jelly sandals with matching shorts, tank tops with Forces and everything in between. A couple girls were walking down the street, from where the houses were, in pajama pants.

Nicotine mixed with Black & Mild smoke filled the air.

"*What's up, baby,*" An old school classic pulled in and did a doughnut in the gravel while the driver spoke to some girls out his window. Bass from his system collided with the music coming from the club.

"*Aye, girl. You fine...*"

Women had on platforms that were too high for them to walk straight. They held onto each other while they wobbled through the lot to get to the door of the club.

"Come on, y'all..." April pulled a bottle of liquor out her purse.

I opened my door slowly and stepped out. Gravel and glass crunched under my feet, giving me a weird feeling in my teeth. I steadied myself in April's heels and looked around the lot.

"Come on."

I adjusted my plastic lime green skirt and sat next to Kendra on the hood of April's vehicle. The lot was packed with cars parked sideways with spinning rims and wheels kicking dust up in the air. Weed smoke singed my nose as a burnt orange Cadillac idled in front of April's ride.

The club was on the corner of a residential area. People spilled out from the houses into the street watching who was leaving the club for the night and who was going in the door where the words "Club 810," was splashed in paint across the side of the building in red.

I took a sip of the drink April poured me and cringed. I wondered why Mom would let me go out of town to stay with someone she'd never met before. I'd only known Kendra for a few months. She didn't know anything about April.

I wish Tori was with me.

Me and Tori always had each other's back. I never had to worry when she was around. The heavy feeling was back in my chest, my heart beating quicker than normal.

I watched ladies old enough to be my mom get in line to go in the club. The crowd going inside was older than the one that was still in the parking lot after the regular bar hours.

"Oohhh girl, look at him…" Kendra grabbed on April's arm.

"We 'bout to get so many numbers!" Morgan said.

I felt out of place. I looked down at my outfit. The lime green hookup April had let me wear looked tacky, and my makeup didn't match.

I hope they don't let me in…

I sipped on my drink. I wished April would have said she was too tired to come out. It didn't make sense because nothing bad had happened, I was kind of having fun, but I couldn't shake the tightness in my chest. I thought April was cool when she had first picked us up. She was funny. But after being around her for a while I started not to like her.

Shoot. I should have called Julian before leaving April's. He would be mad when I got back. I hadn't spoken to him all weekend. I sighed. Julian hated Kendra and didn't want me to come.

"Why you going to Flint?" He'd said with a frustrated look the day I told him I was going with Kendra to visit her sister.

"Just to hang out…"

"You don't even know her sister like that."

Julian thought Kendra was a bad influence. I would tell him he didn't know what he was talking about and that would have him even more upset. Kendra didn't like Julian either. I'd never asked her why. I figured she thought he got in the way of our fun.

"Come on y'all." April hopped off the hood of her car and put the liquor away. "If they ask for your ID say you accidentally left it at home."

I checked my lipstick in April's side mirror and tugged on my skirt. I was scared to get caught trying to get in. What if they called the police on us. We'd all been drinking and April was the only one that was legal. At the same time I was excited about who we might meet if we did get inside. We made it to the front of the line and April stepped to the bouncer.

"Heyyy."

He grunted and April held her hands out and opened her purse.

"Hmph," the bouncer glanced in her bag, then

moved out the way.

"Come *on* y'all," April bounced up and down in the foyer. "It's only 2:30 and it's *already* jumpin' up in here." She must have been trying to distract him from how young we looked.

Morgan paused in front of the door. She was only 14, but she was cute, tall and heavyset. She could do her makeup good, she looked just like her mom, only younger.

"Go on…" The bouncer threw his head, nodding her in.

Kendra smiled and held her arms out to the side. The bouncer patted her waist through her dress. He was big, with thick purple lips and hands like a gorilla. His gaze traveled slowly down her body before he nodded her in. I hoped he didn't touch me.

I stepped forward and sucked on my teeth as he lingered over my legs with his oily black eyes. We were caught. I could tell by the smirk on his face. He knew I was a teenager. He knew we didn't have any business being at a club in the middle of the night. An after hours. I waited for him to call April outside and take us home. I was relieved.

Maybe I shouldn't be hanging out with Kendra…

My heart beat picked up. Like I was reaching the top of a rollercoaster ride, right before a big drop. Just like when I was kicking it with Hannah. I'd gotten used to pushing the racing feeling away, but it was getting harder to ignore.

"Mmm…" The bouncer stepped back and retraced my figure with his beady eyes. He drew his lip into his mouth and patted his hands down my waist, stopping at my hips. I could read the nasty thoughts running through his head. His stench made me nauseous as his hands lingered. Musty oils mixed with sweat and alcohol. I wanted to jerk away, but I was scared. I wanted to run back to the car and hide until the club let out. The way his calloused hands felt through my clothes. Inches away from my skin. I was exposed in April's short lime green skirt. I felt sick. Like the first time Gideon had touched me.

Dirty.

Only this time a line of people was watching from behind. The bouncer's presence was massive. His body blocked me from my friends.

"Go 'head." He finally nodded. His hands taking one last trip down my thighs.

My lip quivered as I stepped forward.

He held the door open with his eyes glued on my

behind as I walked inside the club.

***

The bus lurched forward as we turned the corner onto 60th.

"Y'all *always* have fun!" Ashley said after Kendra got done telling her part of the story.

Cole shook his head and put his books away.

"Whatchu shaking your head about?" I turned in my seat.

His eyes met mine. "You guys really need to be careful."

I turned all the way around and sat up on my knees. "Careful for what?"

"I'm serious." Cole steadied his gaze on me as the bus turned onto East Kentwood's campus. "Y'all hanging out with people you don't know. You could get into trouble. I don't want you getting hurt."

Silence rang in my ears until the sound of my classmates brought me back to the bus.

"Whatever Cole, anyways, when you gon' hang out with us?" Cole was cute. Plus, he was smart. He was a year ahead of us. He helped me with my math homework whenever I needed it.

"I'm not hanging with you and your friend," He motioned towards Kendra. "Y'all crazy."

"Mmmhmm." I rolled my eyes. "You know you wanna hang..." I'd had a crush on Cole since I'd moved to Camelot and started riding the bus, but he was normal, like my other school friends. He was one of the nicest boys in school. I shook thoughts of Cole out of my head. He wasn't interested in me. He probably thought I was a mess. He knew Julian so I couldn't talk to him even if he'd tried.

The doors to the bus opened, and I grabbed my purse off the seat. I wondered about what Kendra had said about Corrine and Cole.

"See y'all later," I said.

I watched Corrine bop down the aisle ahead of me. "Bye guys," she waved. "Have a great day..." She'd hardly said anything while Kendra and I were talking about our weekend.

"Love you, see you later!" Corrine was off the bus, hugging our friends. I didn't know what to think about her.

She's probably fake, I thought. *No one could be that happy.*

***

"Tiffany." Julian called my name.

"Hi babe!" I jumped up from the cafeteria table to give him a hug.

"What is wrong with you, man?" His arms stayed tense at his side.

"What?"

Julian's forehead dimpled. *"Tiffany."*

"Bye, y'all." I grabbed my cinnamon roll as Lisa shot me a sympathetic look. My friends' faces said they knew there was about to be an argument. They looked like they wanted to shake their heads and laugh because it was my fault, but didn't want to make things worse.

"Whatchu mean, 'what?'" Julian and I exited the cafeteria into the crowded hall. "You went out of town and didn't call me all weekend, then you got back and didn't call me?" His voice got higher at the end.

I had never seen Julian angry. Usually he was cracking jokes in the morning with Curtis by the time I got there. He'd make his way around the cafeteria speaking to people, then come find me and watch me finish my breakfast. He didn't mind being at a table full of my friends, even though they'd teased him about being the only guy. They'd talk about him for how much he liked me, he would kiss me in front of them and joke about them not having boyfriends.

Julian was always in a good mood, even around my girl, Maddie.

Maddie swore she didn't like Julian, she would call him ugly and say I could do better. She would only half be joking around. She was rude like that. I'd tell her not to talk about my man that way and rub Julian's bald head just to get on her nerves. Julian would mess with Maddie too, her not liking him didn't bother him.

I leaned against the wall.

"What's up, man?" Tyson walked by, slapping the back of Julian's shoulder.

"Aye man," Julian threw his head up, "How you feel?" He brought Tyson in for a hug. "I'll check you out later." He snapped. "One." Then turned back to face me. His jaw moved as he squared his feet and planted his hands in his pockets. He looked like he was pondering walking off.

"Babe, I was going to call as soon as I got back." I rest my foot against the baseboard.

"But you didn't, though." The corner of his eyes creased.

I didn't know why I didn't talk to Julian, it would

have been easy, April wouldn't have cared if I made a long distance call. I had missed him, but I didn't know what to say with all the chaos going on in the two bedroom apartment. I didn't want it to sound like I was hiding something, and April's house was loud. Julian didn't want to hear about what was going on in Flint, especially about us going to an after hours club, and I didn't want him to get upset. I thought about the guys I was still kicking it with when I was in town. I knew Julian's friends were telling him things about me messing with other people.

"I didn't want your mom to get mad if the phone rang late."

"What time you get back?"

"11:30."

"On a Sunday."

"Bae..." My fingers grazed Julian's arm.

"Your mom shouldn't have let you go." He pulled away.

"Come on..."

"You went to Flint and didn't get back until 11:30 on a Sunday night? You had school in the morning," Julian's eyes narrowed. "That don't make sense, man. I feel like y'all was doing something you ain't have no business doing."

"Stop calling me that."

"What?"

"Stop saying, '*Man*,' I'm your girl."

"I'm saying, *Tiffany*, when you get with your lil' friend I don't know about you."

"We weren't doing anything but kicking it at the house."

"You knew people was worried about you. Why would Kendra's sister bring y'all back so late?"

Julian was asking better questions than mom had.

"April was waiting to get her car from her husband." I left out the part about Kendra inviting some of her guy friends to kick it with us on Sunday until it was time to leave. And that April had cooked and got too drunk to bring us back until she sobered up.

"Man..." Julian shook his head.

"Don't trip."

"Kendra's a bad influence on you."

I huffed, letting my shoulders drop.

"I'm for real. You act different around her. We've

never even gone a day without talking — since the day we met we've been talking daily. Now you're acting like it's not a big deal? What if I had done that to you?" Julian's eyes looked hurt.

"I called you once."

"For two seconds on Sunday. Then you had to go and said you were going to call right back."

"I'm sorry." I stepped on Julian's toes to hug him. "I'm glad I'm back. I did miss you. I just didn't want to be asking to use April's phone over and over."

Julian turned his head. "I missed you too, man."

I leaned in to kiss his cheek and he pulled away. "Don't act like that." I pouted. "You're being rude."

"Because..."

"*Because* what?"

"I was worried about you and you don't care." He stepped away, sliding his hands back in his pockets. "Your mom was worried too when she didn't hear from y'all all day Sunday. You had me blowing your phone up and your moms didn't have any information."

"I'm sorry."

Julian took a breath and ran his hand across his head. "Alright, man." He pulled me close enough to smell the mint on his lips. "Did you have fun, though?"

"It was cool." I told Julian the parts of my weekend that wouldn't make him upset while he walked me the rest of the way to class.

He listened intently. I could see him reading between the lines whenever I mentioned Kendra. "Can you please not do that again?" His features had softened, but I could still hear the uneasiness in his words.

"Alright."

"Especially for your mom, bae. You ain't have to make her worry like that."

I huffed. A familiar feeling of irritation trickled up my spine.

Mom had been mad when we got in late, but I wasn't the one driving. And she was mad she didn't have a way to reach me. That wasn't my fault either. I didn't know April's number and she hadn't asked before I left. How was she going to let me go all the way to Flint, then get mad? How was she going to get mad at me about things I didn't know?

"You promise?"

"Yeah. I promise."

"Cool. I'll check you out after class." Julian let go of

my hand and kissed my cheek.

I waded through the crowded classroom to my desk and dropped my backpack next to my chair. I was going to have to tell Tori about Julian almost catching me up when I got out of school. I could hear Shonda's voice already. *"You need to stop, sister, it's going to backfire on you…"* I almost laughed. Shonda was going to shake her head and Tori was going to say I was a mess. It was all good, as long as Julian didn't know everything that went on in Flint. I sank into the plastic seat and pulled the orange folder I kept my work in out of my backpack.

Maybe I *should* stop acting the way I did, talking to other guys when I went out.

I was relieved Julian and I had made up. I cared about him. I didn't want to be without him at school. I wondered if he was acting, or if he really did love me.

CHAPTER 10

"Good morning!" Corrine bopped down the aisle of our bus.

"What's up Corrine?"

She threw her backpack on the seat across from me and Kendra. "Oh my gosh you guys, I am *too* tired."

"What?" I teased. "You're never tired."

Corrine had been back at East Kentwood for three weeks, she was the most energetic person I had met. Her hair bounced when she spoke, she was always smiling, and she spoke louder than necessary. You couldn't get her to be still. She'd jump from one conversation to the next without stopping.

"I *know.*" Corinne tossed her hair. A fresh, spring scent lingered in the space, a mix of conditioner and body splash. She stuffed her backpack under the bench in front of her, bouncing in her seat. "I accidentally woke up at like, 4:30 this morning. I thought it was time to get up, so I took a shower. My mom came in there, like, *'Corrine, what are you doing?'* I didn't even realize my alarm hadn't gone off. She told me to read my Bible until it was time to go."

I scrunched up my face. "What did you do?"

Corrine leaned, "Girl, I went in there and read my Bible!"

We cracked up, laughing.

"What, you guys?"

"Corrine, you are a mess."

"What?" She had a confused look on her face. "I did read my Bible. It was good, too."

I held my hand over my mouth. "You are crazy."

"Yeah," Nicole laughed, "Who just reads their bible at 4 o'clock in the morning?"

"What guys? I did read my bible, for like, some hours. I learned a lot."

We fell out laughing.

"Next time go back to sleep, fool."

"Whatever guys," Corrinne shook her head, making her curls bounce into her face. "You guys aren't right. So anyways, did I tell you about that one time…?"

Kendra slapped the bench in front of us, cracking up. "Uh-uh, Corrine, next time you wake up two hours early, take your silly butt back to bed!"

"Oh-my-gosh, you guys aren't right. You know I'm not talking back to my momma."

" — Corrine!" Kendra doubled over.

Corrine laughed. *"Listen,* I'm tryna tell you guys about that one time…"

I sat up on my knees and turned around. Cole had a wide smile on his face. He shook his head. His big, mahogany bible was open in his lap. He would pull it out a lot during our ride to school.

"Whatchu doing?"

"Reading Genesis."

"Hmm…"

Cole was so cool. I wished he would talk to me more.

I looked at the pages in his bible upside down. I thought about how Kendra said him and Corrine used to mess with each other. I wondered if he knew that I knew about that, and how everyone was saying Corrine was a ho. Even Julian had said it when I had asked him if he knew her. That was crazy; Julian didn't talk bad about people.

I couldn't see Corrine being like that. I wondered what the truth was.

I folded my hands across the seat and took in the sea of words on the delicate pages. I wondered what Cole thought about me. He was one of the nicest guys at East Kentwood, but he didn't say a lot on our bus rides, besides making sure Kendra and I were safe.

I wondered if he would ever look at a girl like me, or if a reputation would follow me around like it followed Corrine.

***

"What's wrong?"

Julian breathed hard into the phone. "I don't know, man…"

"What is it?" I sunk backwards into our oversized couch cushions and let my knees rock, side to side.

"Just nervous…"

"It's gonna be okay."

"I got a lot riding on this, I don't want nothing messing up my chances…"

Julian had entered a rap battle with Curtis. Him

and his boys were driving to Battle Creek that weekend to perform.

"I promise, it's gonna be okay..."

"I don't know, man…"

There were going to be music executives at the competition and the grand prize was a record deal. For the past couple weeks it was all Julian talked about.

"It's like, I finally got a chance." He breathed. "I just want everything to go how it's supposed to. I gotta rely on my boys … I don't want nobody messing up."

"Why do you think something's gonna go wrong?"

"You know how these fools get when you're depending on them. They swear things is one way until the day of, then you call 'em on it and they act like they don't know what you talking about. I just want everybody to have they lines right. Come correct. Do what they say they gon' do. And we can get this money."

"Mmm…"

"Dang..."

I imagined Julian running his hand across the grain of his head.

"…I need this contract."

I let his words settle. The smell of Mom's Italian casserole wafted through the air. She hummed a gospel song in the kitchen. Pots clanged as she rinsed dishes in the sink and dried them.

"This would change my life."

I sat quietly. "I wish I could come."

He chuckled. "I wish you could too, you my good luck charm. I should kick one of them knuckleheads out to make room in the ride."

Curtis was driving down with an entourage of their friends from school and some of Julian's cousins.

I giggled. "They'd really call you whipped, then."

"I don't care. I want you there more than them." Julian hummed over a beat.

"Don't worry about it, you're always rappin'." I teased. "You just gotta do what you always do."

He laughed. "I know…"

I thought about how he'd rap early in the morning while I finished my breakfast. He'd let me eat the outside of my cinnamon roll, then steal the gooey part in the middle with all the frosting.

"You gotta make sure you call me as soon as y'all win."

"Babe…"

"Hmm?"

"Lemme ask you something."

I let the silence linger.

"Do you cheat on me?"

My heart started beating fast. "No." I responded quicker than I should.

"Hmph…"

"Why?"

"Because, my boys be telling me things."

"Things like what?"

"Just things, man..."

I had seen some of Julian's friends at a party me and Kendra went to the weekend before. I shouldn't have been surprised they told him. I wondered if they saw me give my number to one of the guys.

"There you go, calling me 'man.' "

"You know how I talk."

"I'm not cheating, bae."

Julian paused. "Good."

Commercials from his television filled the space for several seconds and I drew my feet up under me and rested my head. I loved being on the phone with Julian. He was like a warm blanket. It was the most comfortable place I could be. I could be myself with him. I should have been able to be myself with him. I wish I didn't have a reason to lie.

"I'mma definitely call you when the rap battle is over." Julian hesitated. "You think we got a chance at the deal?"

"Y'all are good. You got a chance."

"Thanks, bae." His voice lightened. "So should I wear my leather bomber? Or I could wear my suede jacket with the fur around the collar since it matches my Tims..."

***

"Good Morning!" Corrine walked towards me and Kendra down the aisle.

"Hi Corrine." We said in unison. I was tired every morning, but Corrine was always full of energy, and ready to tell us about it.

"Oh my gosh, you guys. Did I tell you about my new job? I work at McDonalds." She threw her backpack. "The one at the mall. You should seriously come visit me at work, I love my job, I can hook y'all up if you want me to, all you gotta do is…"

"Dang," I whispered in Kendra's ear. "This girl never shuts up." I laughed.

"Girl." Kendra rolled her eyes. She turned. "What are you doing this weekend Corrine?"

"Nothing yet. I don't have any plans." She got comfortable in her seat.

"We're going out if you wanna roll." Kendra said.

"Ohhh, cool, where you guys going?"

"We'll probably just hook up with some of my friends, it's bound to be a party somewhere."

"Aww, I wish I could, but no thanks. My mom has me cleaning the *whole* house this weekend, and you know how my mom is, girl. It's gonna to take forever."

"Hey Cole," Corrine swiveled in her seat. "Did you get the answers to that pre-test? I really need to study cuz you know how I am with math…"

Kendra switched positions in her seat and closed her eyes. "So anyways, girl. I talked to that tall dude I met a couple weekends ago, Mark. You remember Mark don't you? He said he wants to hook up, but I don't know…"

I tuned Kendra out, I was thinking about Corrine.

She obviously wanted to be around us. She sat with us every morning on the bus and found us at lunch time. I couldn't figure out why she never wanted to hang.

How does she have a reputation?

CHAPTER 11

"Heyyy, girl..."

I laughed before Tori could get her words all the way out. We had a secret language. Just by the way she said hello when I picked up the phone I could tell something was going down.

"What's up?"

"Your mom told my mom she was going out of town. What we doin'?" Tori whispered. "Shonda finna be here in a minute."

"Dang..."

"What's wrong?"

"Julian made plans for us before I knew my mom was leaving."

"Aww, girl, have fun."

"You want me to cancel?"

"Nah, hang out with your man." Tori said in her regular voice. "We can do something tomorrow. Julian staying the night with you?"

Mom was going to Chicago for the weekend. Most of our extended family lived there. She only got a chance to go when someone in our family died. One of her sisters would call, and Mom would exclaim, *"Lord, have mercy."*

That would let me know she had to leave.

She was frantic that day when I got home from school. She didn't want me home by myself, but didn't have the money for both of us to take the three-hour bus trip. She would always be torn. Mom was the youngest out of 11 so she had nieces and nephews that were older than her. I hardly knew her family outside of my little baby cousin, so I never wanted to go to Chicago unless it was for a family reunion, or an event where I could have fun. I didn't want to go to a funeral with people that were strangers to me. When Mom left she usually sent me to Tori's.

"No," I made a face. "I wish. Rodney's coming here to check on me. I'll stay here tonight. I'll stay at your house tomorrow night. You sure you don't want me to cancel?"

"Me and Shonda ain't going nowhere. We just gon' watch movies ... ooohhh, matter of fact, me and Shonda gon' come by there and grab your stereo. What time y'all leaving?"

"Probably around 7:00."

"Don't do anything I wouldn't do." Tori sang.

I laughed. "Shut up."

***

"Where you think we should live when I get this record deal, boo? Atlanta, or LA?"

"Boy, you are crazy." I covered my mouth so I didn't spit my food out.

"I'm serious..." Julian laughed as our waiter came to check on our drinks. We were at Friday's. Waitresses rushed around the busy restaurant taking orders. The black and white stripes on their shirts reminded me of referees.

Julian clacked his tongue against the roof of his mouth. "You tryna tell me when I make it big you ain't gon' want my money?"

"Julian, stop!"

"Answer the question, boo." He grinned.

"Ain't nobody with you for your money."

Julian's mom had dropped him off, then we'd walked the 15 minutes it took to get to the mall. Mom was already out of town.

"Watch," Julian bit into his chicken strip. "When I blow up you 'gon be mad at yourself for doubting me."

"Alright, let's live in Atlanta. That way I can go to Spelman and get my business degree."

Julian and his boys had made it to the second round of the rap battle, but they didn't win. I felt bad for him. They had been telling the same stories about it at school all week.

"Boo, I was standing on the stage, right. I'm all in it— you know how I usually am—jumping up and down..."

Julian had replayed the performance for me like he was shadow boxing.

"When they called the next round, I'm over here, off to the side," He'd showed me how he was standing. *"...And Curtis was right next to me. I had my head down 'cause I knew they was gon' pick us, but I didn't wanna be looking at the crowd when they called our name..."* Julian had filled me in on the whole day. How they were rappin' on stage, how hype the crowd was...how they should have won the whole battle. They got to meet people from the

recording label and take pictures.

"Alright, we can go to Atlanta." Julian cheesed. "I'm serious Tiffany, I'mma make it big and you gon' be my wife. I'mma take care of you." He reached for my hand. "We gon' have a little boy and everything."

I pulled away and crossed my arms in front of me.

"You think I'm playin'," he laughed, "We gon' name him little Julian."

We talked about having a baby a lot. I didn't take him seriously though. He acted like he wanted me to get pregnant right then.

"And what if we have a girl?"

"Nah boo, I know we gotta have a boy first…"

Our waitress set raspberry lemonade in front of us.

"Why?"

"Cuz, I'mma man."

"Boy, that don't make sense…" Sometimes I liked the way Julian talked about us. He made me feel special, like we'd always be together. I'd secretly hope I was pregnant every month so he'd have to stay around and I'd have a baby I could love.

"You're 17," I said, "Why you always talking about

having a family?"

"I *been* wanting a family, I've always wanted that."

"You don't know you want to be with me forever."

"I know what I want. I know I want a family, and I'mma be a good dad."

"Yeah, but *how* do you know?"

"I don't know…" Julian got the same intense look in his eyes he got the first time he told me he loved me. "I guess since my dad ain't never been around I always said I was gon' have a family…I said I was gon' have kids and be around for my lil shortys.

He put his fork down and pushed his plate away. "…I said I was gonna be the type of man he never was for me."

Julian paused while I played with the crumpled up napkin on the table.

"I ain't asking you to marry me, man, I'm just asking for a commitment. I know I love you Tiffany, that's not gonna change."

"Mmm…" I took his hand and looked away. Sometimes I couldn't stand him. He was a junior in high school, only one year ahead of me. No boy in high school wanted to have a family. Sometimes I'd pick a fight with him for no reason. When he'd call I'd say I was busy and get off the phone just so I could hear him get upset. I didn't understand why he loved me. I wanted him to prove, no matter what I did, he wouldn't leave. I didn't care what he said, or how good he treated me, I felt like he would leave...because everybody left.

"I'm done with my food," Julian said, "You ready, boo?"

"Yeah, I'm ready."

I thought back to middle school. And the summer after 8th grade. I was too much like Hannah to just be with Julian...and too used to being "loved" by people like Gideon.

I pushed the thought away as Julian grabbed our to-go boxes.

CHAPTER 12

"H*ey girrrrl.*"
"Hey *Kendraaa*." Me and Kendra bust out laughing.

For Kendra and I not to have known each other long it was weird how we clicked. Almost like me and Tori. I could tell she had something up by her tone.

"You so stupid." I cradled the phone against my shoulder.

Kendra whispered. "*Girl*, whatchu doing tonight?" It sounded like she was cupping the phone. That was different since she didn't get in trouble for anything we got into. Her Mom didn't mind what she did. She just had to be in the house at a reasonable hour. Or let her mom know if she was staying out all night. Her best friend Amber's parents didn't mind if Kendra stayed over there. Since Amber was in her first year of college she didn't have a curfew.

I giggled. "I don't have plans."

"You gotta come with me, girl. I want you and one of my boys from Flint to meet."

"Who?"

"You ever heard me talk about my boy, Johnny?"

"I don't think so."

"His cousin's name is Caine. You'll like him. Let me make some calls, we'll pick you up."

***

Caine was fine. His thick, rope-sized braids were plaited to the back and stuck out from under a dingy, gray beanie. His hunter green Carhartt jacket and khaki colored Dickies fit perfectly, one size bigger than he needed. His dark lips were almost purple with a hint of pink left over in the middle from his regular skin tone.

I could tell Caine and his cousins smoked a lot. Their car smelled like they could take a thousand showers and still smell like weed, and purple blunt papers, and the sweet, woodsy scent of Black & Milds, and cherry air freshener trees from their Cadillac, all swirled into one intoxicating scent.

Caine glanced in the rear view mirror.

He'd ignored me when I got in the Cadillac. It was a little after 11:30 and I'd had to close the door quietly so Mom didn't hear me leave. I'd shut the door and ran to their ride, trying to avoid the soft glow of the street lamps by our townhouse so none of my neighbors would see me leaving. I'd wondered whose car it was. I'd never seen guys our age drive that kind of car. It was cold, like it didn't know how to get warm, and ran with a stutter, but it was a Caddy. I'd wondered how old Caine was. He didn't look that much older than me, but the deadpan, contemplative look he gave made me think he was years older. I'd absentmindedly fingered the door handle, tracing the lines of the lock, trying to find the best place to lay my gaze.

"This my girl, Tiffany..."

Caine didn't respond when Kendra had introduced me to him and Johnny, he looked like I was interrupting their vibe. His eyes were tight and his head was low. He'd thrown his head up, withdrawn, and Kendra filled the space talking to Johnny about what was popping off in their hometown, Flint.

Minutes passed and I made myself busy looking at the wintery streets pass by out the window. I didn't go to the hood much. The houses got older as we drove deeper into the city. There was a Walgreens on the left and a church on the right, we made a turn and passed a large park with abandoned swings that looked like they'd make a creaking sound if you pushed hard enough. I craned my neck to look at the street sign. The area looked familiar.

"Your girl's kinda cute." Caine shot a look at Kendra. He held a blunt to his lips, licked the paper, and rolled.

Kendra laughed. "Boy, *all* my friends are cute."

"Yeah, ok…" Caine turned the music up loud enough to block my thoughts out. Even though Johnny had picked us up it felt like Caine was the one driving. He wet his lips slowly, rolling his weed.

Kendra clacked her sparkly acrylic nails across the headrest the way girls did after they first got them done and wanted you to notice. "Uh-uh, Caine. All my friends are pretty." Her voice was high pitched, laughter dancing through each note.

Caine chuckled. "I said, 'yeah.' " His tone was low and gravelly, amused. I started thinking of ways to tell Kendra I shouldn't be there.

I should leave… I wanted to ask Johnny to take me back. I didn't want Caine to be irritated that they had picked me up. I could tell he wasn't feeling me. Maybe he had a girlfriend and didn't want to be seen out. Or maybe he thought I was too young to be hanging with them.

Johnny pulled up to a convenience store. He threw the car in park, got out and stretched, making a groaning sound as his back cracked.

"Aye, y'all want anything?" He turned.

"Whatchu getting?" Kendra said.

"Something to drink on. Some Henny..." Johnny bent down in the window and rubbed his hands together. "It's cold as hell. Whatchu want?"

"Get us some Boone's Farm."

"That's all?"

"Yeah," Kendra took her seatbelt off and leaned over the driver's seat. "Caine, let me see what CDs yall be listening to."

"You want anything, Tiff?"

I shook my head. I didn't want Johnny to spend money on me.

Johnny blew in his hands and jogged towards the store.

"Get strawberry!" Kendra called out the window.

"Strawberry, what?"

"Boone's Farm!"

"Alright." He slowed, walking backwards.

"And get some ice!"

Johnny smirked, shaking his head before snatching the door to the tiny convenience store open. He liked Kendra. Caine liked her too, as a friend. I was imposing on them.

I dipped my head in the backseat, tracing a circle in the frosted over glass, like making myself smaller would make me invisible. *I should leave.*

I was starting not to like hanging with Kendra. Going out with her reminded me of tagging along with Hannah when I was younger. I never knew exactly what I was getting into and I never felt all the way comfortable.

Caine looked at me in the mirror and took a long hit of his blunt. "Cute…"

CHAPTER 13

"So what's up?"

"With...?" I rest the phone between my shoulder and my ear.

"Don't play dumb."

"With what, Caine?"

"With me and you," he said, "I want you to be mine."

"I..."

"Why you stuttering, Tiff? Is it that hard to say yes?"

"Caine..." His name slid off my lips like honey.

"Just say 'yes.' "

Caine and I had been hanging since Kendra introduced us. We'd been going back and forth about hooking up since the first night they'd picked me up.

I was excited Caine wanted me. At the same time, I didn't know what to do. I was used to Tori's friends that I'd kick it with, like Blaque. He didn't try to get me to break up with Julian. He didn't care. Caine was making demands.

"You know I got a boyfriend, Caine."

"But yet you talkin' to me."

Kendra was right. Caine was my type. Aggressive and pushy. He reminded me of Gideon. His quiet intensity - I could close my eyes and think back to when I was in Breton Court sitting on Dad's stoop, waiting on Gideon to show up.

"Just because I got a man, don't mean I can't have friends."

"Hmph…"

Gideon had taught me what I knew. *"Don't say no…"*

That's what he'd say when his weight was crashing down on top of me when I was 14. When he'd come to my house on Wednesday nights when Mom went to church I'd want to say, "no." I wanted to be a normal girlfriend and boyfriend that had fun together and talked and laughed. Gideon would act like he wanted to hang out, but within minutes he'd be telling me to go to my room. If I acted like I didn't want to have sex he'd

RESTORE | A LOST GIRL'S JOURNEY TO HOPE

get upset. Even though I hated Gideon, I'd listened to everything he told me.

"Don't say no…"

Now I had Julian and he wasn't enough, and "no" wasn't in my vocabulary. I told all the guys I dealt with I had a boyfriend. I'd tell them I loved Julian to see if they cared. It didn't matter to them.

It didn't make sense, I knew Caine didn't care about me. He probably had a lot of girls he dealt with. I'd never seen him with anyone, but the way he acted, I could tell he was with other chicks when he wasn't with me. Nobody told me, but I could tell. He was the type of dude that would never let you find out all the stuff he had going on. I just wanted him to really want me. I wanted him to keep trying to get me to be with him so I could feel important, but he wasn't serious, and I was trying to wait him out. Caine just wanted to have sex with me. I wanted him to want me for more than that. I was addicted to the feeling of *almost* being loved.

I wanted Caine to start having feelings for me and really want me for who I was. If he went from hardly paying me any attention to really being interested in me, that would make me feel special. I didn't feel special having a regular boyfriend. I had Julian but I craved someone new wanting me all the time. I was like a dope fiend.

"Why you still got your little boyfriend anyways?" Caine inhaled and I imagined smoke enveloping his maple skin. It felt like deja vu, sitting in Dad's old apartment on the phone with Gideon, waiting on him to tell me when he was coming over. "You talkin' to me every night when you get off the phone with him, but you call yourselves being together..." He chuckled. "You know you want me. You might as well break up with him."

"Boy..." I laughed Caine off. Julian loved me. Caine was like everybody else. He didn't know how to love.

"How old is that dude?"

"16..."

"Where he work?"

"Caine."

"Where he work? He gotta job, right? He keeps you laced, buys you anything you want..." Sarcasm filtered through his tone.

"It's not about that."

"Where do he work?"

"The skating rink."

"Aww, man."

"Stop…"

"I can give you whatever you want, but you wanna mess with a little kid?" Caine and his cousins didn't hide what they did to get money. They pushed weight. When they weren't selling dope, they were robbing someone's spot. They had one of my friends from school running for them. Deacon. I had met Deacon when we were still in the 9th grade. He was a hot head. The shortest dude, but always into it with somebody. He was funny though, and he was quick to back up what he said. He got in a couple fights when we were in ninth grade, but I hadn't seen him much since sophomore year started.

"Make it make sense." Caine taunted me.

Deacon would set up dealers for Caine and his cousins to rob. Since he'd started hanging with Caine I barely saw him at school.

"I can give you what you want and you running behind a kid."

"You're not that much older."

"But I can give you what you want. And my mindset is grown."

"You don't even *know* what I want," I teased. "You barely even know me."

"I know what you want," Caine's gravelly voice

weighed on my thoughts like bricks.

The tension that had started in my heart spread across my chest and into my gut.

I need to get off the phone…

That thought made sense to me. I didn't need Caine when I already had Julian.

"Whatever Caine … you don't want me." I didn't know why I was hesitant about being with him. He wasn't the first guy I'd cheated with. The same thing that scared me about Caine made me excited to be around him. There was just something about him that threw me off.

"You gon' be mine."

I wasn't breaking up with Julian. Julian loved me. Caine didn't know anything about love. Caine was Gideon.

Maybe that's what I liked about him. He was familiar to me. Caine was comfortable to me, like getting in your own bed at night. He didn't have to say much of anything to me. It was like I 'knew' him.

"Keep acting like I ain't serious—"

I giggled. "Chill out."

"It's all good, shorty." Ice clinked against glass in

the background. "Keep seeing your man...you gon' have regrets."

***

I let my legs dangle over the edge of Tori's couch. I was trying to find something to watch.

"Put on some videos." Tori called from the kitchen.

I landed on MTV and the intro to LL Cool J's "Hey Lover" filled the screen.

"Heyyy, that's my song!" Tori came into the living room, grabbed the remote and danced around the coffee table. She'd been in the kitchen washing dishes.

I jumped up and moved my hips.

"Hey..." Tori cat-walked the length of the couch and back like she was the girl in the video.

"You so stupid." I laughed.

"Hey Lover..." She sang along to the hook.

"This my new favorite video." I sang as L lifted weights on the screen. His muscles were ripped.

"Girl, his lips. He needs to stop licking 'em. He is so fine."

"I know."

Tori danced around the room with the remote, holding it to her face like she was inches from L's lips.

"You so crazy." I threw a pillow after her.

"Girl, he is fine. Mmm."

The song ended and she went back in the kitchen to finish cleaning up. I changed stations to BET just as Real Love by Mary J. Blige came on. I stood up and rocked left and right the way MJ did in all her videos. "Go Mary…"

"Ayyye, Ayyye." Tori waved a dish rag as she finished her chores.

I giggled and fell back onto the couch.

"You wanna go to the mall?" She asked, coming back into the living room.

"Yeah, we can go."

"Bet, we can get something to wear for tomorrow."

"Where we going?"

"I don't know. But we're going somewhere." She cheesed.

I laughed. "Ok."

"Cool, I'll call Shae and see if she wants to come."

"With her crazy self." I kicked my feet back up on the sofa.

"Whatchu gonna wear?"

"Let me look through your closet."

"Alright." She said getting up. "I need to wash clothes."

It was Friday after school. It would be a cold walk to the mall but it wasn't far.

"I'm surprised Julian ain't trying to hang out with you tonight." Tori teased.

"He has to work."

"Aww, he's always working. That's good." She flipped through the stations.

"Yup. That means I can get some numbers tonight and see him tomorrow."

"Oooohhh," Tori threw a cushion at my shoulder.

"Haaa," I ducked.

"You are bad."

I picked at the chipped polish on my nails. "I just keep my options open. "

"Mmm-mm-mm." Tori shook her head.

"I'm just playing, I'm just playing. I love him."

"Yeah, ok." She said, giving me a big sister look.

"What?" I laughed.

"Nothing." Tori beamed. Come on, lemme call Shae and we can go."

CHAPTER 14

"Hey Tiff, wait up!" I slowed down so Kendra could catch up to me and Julian. It was 2:23 and he was walking me to the lot between the east side of campus and the freshman building where the buses met.

I stopped. "What's up, girl?"

"*This* chick..." Julian rolled his eyes. He stretched, swinging his arms upward, impatiently cracking his neck side to side.

"Boy," Kendra winced in his direction. "Anyways," She turned back to me. "Don't get on the bus, I got a ride for us." Her eyes lit up, like they did when she had a plan.

"...Can't *stand* this chick." Julian mumbled.

"Bae…" I shot him a look. I didn't want him and

Kendra exchanging words in the parking lot.

I turned back to Kendra. "For real? With who?" I hated riding the bus. It took 45 minutes to get to our stop, and I still had a 10 minute walk home.

"Johnny and Morgan and them…" Kendra gave me a pointed look.

"Pssh…" Julian breathed out, hard.

Kendra smirked. " — Whatever."

I shook my head. "Y'all stop." Kendra and Julian had been getting into it since we went to Flint. Anytime she said something Julian would have something smart to say and vice versa. It got on my nerves. As good of a boyfriend as Julian was Kendra shouldn't have had anything to say. She acted like Julian had done something to me. He had never gotten caught up cheating. He took me anywhere I wanted to go, she had no reason not to like him.

Kendra flipped her hair. "Anyways, you coming?"

"Bet," I glanced at Julian, "I'll be over there in a minute."

Kendra switched the arm carrying her purse. "Come on," she yelled over her shoulder. "They're in the west lot. You gotta hurry before they leave."

Kids filed past me to get to their buses. I glanced at my watch. 2:29.

"Alright babe, I'mma go with Kendra. I'll call you when I get home." I kissed Julian.

He kept his hands in his pockets. "Who y'all riding with?"

I tapped my foot. "Just some of Kendra's friends." I knew who was in the car. I was geeked. Johnny and Caine were always together. Caine and his cousins must have come up to the school during our last hour to get Deacon. I hadn't seen Caine in days. I wondered if he was still mad at me for not breaking up with Julian when he asked me to.

Julian ran his hand across his head. "Naw babe..."

"What?"

"Get on the bus."

I screwed up my face. "Whatchu mean?"

"I'm serious, Tiffany." He stopped in front of me. "Get on the bus, man."

"For what?" I turned up my lip. "I don't want to take the bus if I got a ride, it takes forever for us to get home. We gotta drop all them kids off."

Julian's jaw moved the way it did when he was

getting angry. "I'm serious."

"Julian…"

"Just listen —"

"Listen to what? Why you acting like it's a big deal for me to get a ride?"

"Come on man," Julian's voice softened. He reached for my hand. "I got a bad feeling, just get on the bus."

I huffed. "Why?" I stood on my toes, looking towards the west wing to see if I could still see Kendra. If I didn't hurry Caine would leave.

Julian looked up. "I'm not sure why, I just do."

"Well, then it shouldn't matter."

He ran his forefinger across my hand. "Tiffany…"

"What's the big deal?"

"I just want you to get on the bus…"

Julian wasn't stupid. If he didn't know who Caine was, he'd heard rumors about me. His friends had seen me hanging out with other guys.

I crossed my arms in front of my chest. "I'm getting a ride home."

A boy bumped into me with his backpack. "My

bad…"

The buses started rumbling ahead of us.

"Julian." I pleaded. I wanted to just leave, but I didn't want Julian getting upset. We'd been getting into a lot of small arguments. He thought I was going out too much on weekends when he wanted to spend time with me. I wanted him to come over during the week after school. We couldn't agree. He thought I was choosing Kendra over him. I wasn't choosing anyone, I just wanted to have fun. I wanted him to understand and spend time with me when I wanted him to. He'd started ignoring me when I didn't give in.

Julian kicked at the gravel. "Just get on the bus, Tiffany…" He looked up and I started forward, confused.

Tears were in his eyes.

Black exhaust from the idling buses filled my nose. My bus driver swung her handle. "Time to go!" She rapped on the windshield.

I took one last look toward the west lot. "Fine."

"You goin' home?"

I rolled my eyes. "Yeah."

"Bet, I love you." Julian leaned in to kiss me.

***

I put my key in the front door. The phone rang inside the house, startling me. I wiggled the key free and let my backpack fall on the tile floor in the hallway just as I heard Mom's voice on the answering machine kick in.

"Hi, you've reached the St. John's residence, I'm sorry we're not here to answer your call —"

"Hello?" I picked up, out of breath. A dial tone hummed in my ear.

Shoot. I hated missing calls. I was irritated from my walk home. The bus ride was boring. Kendra wasn't there, so I didn't have anybody to share stories with. Julian was getting on my nerves being so overprotective. *Get on the bus.* He didn't know we were getting a ride with Caine, he might have assumed we were doing something wrong, but he didn't have anything to be worried about. My friends were hanging out with Caine and I was stuck at home.

Ring Ring Ring!

I flinched, almost dropping the receiver. Whoever was calling wanted to talk, bad.

"Hello —"

"Oh my God, oh my God, oh my God…" The voice

on the line made my heart freeze.

"Kendra?" I stepped forward, hands trembling.

"Oh my God, oh my God!"

"Kendra?" My heart raced, trying to place the voice.

"Tiffany, we gotta get help ... help ... we gotta get ... oh my God ... oh my God, oh my God..." Kendra's voice went in and out.

I steadied myself against the couch. "Kendra, what's wrong?"

"Oh my God, oh my God..." The call broke up. Distorted. "...I can't believe this ... we gotta..." Her voice echoed as though she pulled the phone away from her ear, *"We gotta get help y'all. We gotta find him!"*

"Kendra!"

Screaming pierced my eardrum.

"Kendra, what's going on?"

"Oh my God Tiffany, this is crazy —"

"What?"

"Oh my God."

" — What is it?"

"I don't know what to do..."

"Kendra, you're talking too fast. What's wrong?"

"We gotta get help, they got Deacon!"

"Who?" My mind worked hard to register what she was saying. Caine and Johnny were at the school earlier. They had to have picked Deacon up.

"They had guns—"

"*Who?*"

"Johnny and Caine! Everybody!!!"

Blood rushed to my ears.

"They took us to this house —"

I staggered. "Where are you?"

" — on the North side."

"Kendra who had guns?"

"We was chillin' and then these dudes came…" Commotion picked up around Kendra in the background — people hollering and screaming. *"We gotta get help!"*

"Kendra, calm down, I can't hear you."

Men's voices. Yelling.

"Caine and them pulled out their guns…we had to hide in the closet…" She put the phone down. *"Oh my God, Oh my God, Oh my God…Morgan, we gotta help him!*"

"Kendra!"

"What!"

"Tell me what happened! Tell me!"

"They — the other guys," she panted, "they were bangin' on the door, yelling and —"

"And what?"

"They took him! They got Deacon!" she screamed.

I staggered backwards. Gripping air.

"We don't know where he is! They sent Deacon to go rob these dudes. They had guns! They said they ain't giving him back unless … oh my God, oh my God, oh my God…"

My hand trembled around the phone as I fought the urge to scream. I had to do something. I needed to call for help.

"Breathe, Kendra. Where are you?"

Static filled the receiver.

"Kendra!"

Metal scraped against hard plastic. "Kendra!"

Kendra's voice sounded muffled, underwater. "I

don't know!"

Where's Caine?

"I don't know the address." The phone clattered to the ground. *"We gotta get help!"*

I gripped the receiver, tight. My heart beat fast. I whipped around, searching the living room. I had to get help. I didn't know how.

"Kendra…" I started.

"Oh my God, oh my God," Kendra's voice was raspy from screaming.

"Kendra, tell me where you are."

"I don't know."

" Where —"

"There's nothing here! No furniture. Nothing. Nothing." Her voice faded out. *"We gotta help Deacon. Where'd they go?"*

I searched the room. My eyes fixed on the phone books under the end table. I scrambled to drag them onto the couch.

"Kendra, did you see anything when you got there? A business? Do you know the apartment's name?" I needed a way to help find them. To tell 911.

"Kendra?"

Mens voices. My chest tightened. A ball of fear growing in my stomach. Threatening to explode.

"Oh my God, oh my God, oh my God ... why would they take him?"

"Kendra!"

Yelling. Banging on metal. *Boom boom, boom boom boom.* As though a door might give way.

My friends.

"Kendra?"

Don't let them die, don't let them die...

More voices. Louder and louder. *Caine.*

"Kendra!"

"What are we gonna do?"

"Kendra?"

Fear bubbled over, spilling into my lungs. I fought to breathe. *I gotta get help.*

"Oh my God, oh my God..."

Julian's voice echoed in my head. *Get on the bus.*

"Kendra!"

CHAPTER 15

"Why you gotta hang with girls who are out of control, Tiffany?"

"How is Kendra out of control?"

"You know what I mean." I imagined spit leaving Julian's mouth.

I switched shoulders cradling the receiver.

"Y'all act like you don't got no sense when y'all together. Last time you went to Flint, you ain't come back to school till Tuesday."

"That wasn't my fault."

"I didn't say it was your fault."

"Why you complaining then?"

"I'm not complaining, I'm asking you to think!"

Me, Kendra, and Morgan had gone to visit April again, a couple months after Christmas break. April got into it with her husband that weekend — something about one of them cheating on the other one. We went to Club 810 Saturday night; the parking lot was just as bad as before. People were smoking weed and drinking out in the open.

Some guys we had met at the club came back to the apartment and stayed with us, along with this dude Morgan had been kickin' it with. That Sunday morning April got a phone call. She went out the house early, cussing out whoever she was on the phone with. When she got back she was breathing hard. Her car was scratched up and her tires were slashed. We had to wait until Monday night for one of Kendra's boys to get off work and take us home.

"That wasn't Kendra's fault either —"

"You gon' mess your grades if you keep missing school. You need to chill out on Kendra. I'm telling you, man..."

"Julian…"

"Naw, don't 'Julian' me. I'm for real."

"Julian…"

"What, Tiffany?" He spit my name. "You don't never listen to nobody."

I paused to give myself time to gather my thoughts. "You making things bigger than what they are. My grades don't have nothin' to do with Kendra."

I felt like I was spiraling into a ditch. My grades were slipping. Instead of A's and B's like I normally got I was barely passing half my classes. Trying to stay out late with Kendra and kicking it with Tori on the weekends was making it hard to stay caught up on my homework and caught up with Julian.

Julian paused. "Are you cheating on me, Tiffany?"

I smacked my lips. "No."

"I be hearing stuff about you, man…"

"You believe the stuff you hear?"

"Naw, but don't *make* me believe it!"

"I'm not cheating on you Julian, just because I'm hangin' with Kendra doesn't mean I'm cheating. Stop feedin' into what people say."

Julian had been trippin' about Kendra for weeks. He couldn't stand her. He thought all the bad stuff he was hearing about me was her fault. He'd been telling me to leave Kendra alone before Deacon had even gotten taken.

Get on the bus.

I almost lost it the day Kendra called me, stuck in Caine's apartment.

I didn't have any idea where she was or how to get help to her. There was nothing I could do but hold the phone and listen to her scream.

Kendra and Morgan made it out the closet. Kendra didn't want me to call the police because they would have all gone down, but we were worried about Deacon. We didn't find out what happened to him until the following week. He came back to school that Tuesday, cut up from head to toe.

"Deacon!" We jumped up to hug him when he limped into the cafeteria that morning.

"What's up y'all..." We didn't know what to do when Deacon got taken. We'd thought he was dead. And calling the police meant telling on Johnny, Caine and their cousins. We were stuck.

"I'm good, I'm good..." We'd gathered around him. He'd gotten thrown through a window and pistol whipped. But he was ok. I was relieved he was alive.

The crazy thing was, I was even more drawn to Caine.

I didn't know why. He was exciting. Dangerous. Like Gideon. The fact that Gideon made me have sex with him when we were together didn't make me less confused about wanting him to be with just me.

I'd wanted him to change and love me. To let me know I was worth more than what he was doing to me.

Caine's presence was the same. He was an unknown to me. I wasn't sure if he was really feeling me and that made me want him to pursue me more. He was a drug dealer, but that hadn't affected me. At least not yet.

I wasn't in danger when my friends were stuck in the closet, but I could have been. That made me want Caine to draw closer. To find out how exciting things could get. My friends had made it out ok, but I was stuck at home, safe from harm. Home was where I should have wanted to be. Safe. With Julian.

"I trust you." Julian breathed deep, "I just want you to think before you act. You're gonna end up in trouble."

Julian checked up on me more than Mom did. He hadn't found out about Caine, but our arguments about me coming and going were getting more intense. He wasn't buying my lies about me staying out late because I forgot my keys, or not having a ride home at night.

"Stop letting people mess with your head."

"Yeah, man..."

"I'm serious."

"You better be. I'm serious too."

"I wouldn't even do you like that, Julian. Your friends be making up stuff just to make you angry."

Julian loved me, but he knew his friends weren't lying to him. They saw me out, kicking it with Tori while he was at work. Julian couldn't stand Kendra, but he loved Tori. Probably because she liked how we were together — she'd tell him that every time we all kicked it. Me and Tori had fun when we went out, but she wanted me to calm down and just be with Julian. She liked how sweet he was, and how he never gave up on me. Julian didn't think Tori was perfect, but he knew she'd always look out for me. He thought maybe when it came down to it, she'd tell me the right thing to do.

"I love you, bae."

"Yeah, I love you too, man..."

"Stop saying it like that."

"I love you, Tiffany. You know I love you."

I wanted to love him, but I didn't know how. My love was broken.

***

"...Ok Tiffany, I want you to stay at Tori's house at night. There's food in the kitchen," Mom rushed through the house packing her things, "And these are the numbers where you can reach me at your aunt's." She handed me a piece of paper. "If no one answers, leave a message, they'll make sure it gets to me." She put her hand to her head. Her face was flushed. "Lord, have mercy…" She tapped the refrigerator.

"What Mom?"

She looked around the kitchen.

"Where is my purse…"

"Right here." I handed an oversized purse that looked like a piece of luggage to her off the table.

"Jesus," she scooped it up, looking through the contents. "And I still need to do something to my hair…"

The bags under Mom's eyes made her look old. It was Wednesday night. She'd just gotten a call from her sisters.

"I'll leave a little bit of money on top of the refrigerator, in case you need anything."

Her aunt, my great aunt had died. Mom was leaving for Chicago on Friday.

"If I had the money I'd get a ticket for you to go, too." Lines creased her eyebrows and she stopped packing. "You really shouldn't be here alone."

"I'm alright, Mom." I didn't want her to get so

worried that she called one of my brothers to come stay with me. "I'll be at Tori's most of the time."

"You *still* shouldn't be here alone..." She shook her head and kept packing.

I waited for her to go to Bible study to call Tori.

"Hello?" She answered on the first ring.

"Hellooo," I sang. "Guess what? I got the house to myself this weekend!"

"I know! My mom just told me."

"Ayyye, we 'bout to have fun."

"What we getting into?"

"You already know," I laughed. "We *gotta* have a party."

"Bet," Tori said, "Let me start calling people... oooh, you know what?"

"What's up?"

"We should have a card party Friday night—just us from the neighborhood."

We had some guy friends we chilled with in our complex. They were like their own gang. They played basketball and smoked the day away. We always talked about how trifling they were, but we'd been cool with them since we were younger. We had fun together when we were getting along well enough to hang out. Sometimes they'd start feeling themselves and act like they liked us, but they were more like brothers.

"Okay," I said. "We can bust some spades."

"Right. But Shonda gotta be one of our partners. I still don't know what I'm doing."

I laughed. "You so stupid."

"Yup," I could picture her nodding her head. "We can cook and everything—then we can have the real party Saturday night."

"This weekend is gon' be off the *chain*. I'mma call Kendra, you call Shonda."

"Cool, I'll call her right now. I'll be over there later."

CHAPTER 16

"You know my mom leaves tomorrow … you hanging with us this weekend?"

"I can't bae, I gotta work."

"Awww…"

"I can kick it with you before I go in."

I pouted. "You hardly make time for me," I teased. Julian hadn't been able to kick it with me long the last time Mom went out of town, his mom wasn't buying it. I didn't want to be at the house by myself. My girls would be there but I was starting to miss Julian. Since I hadn't been going out of town we'd made up and were getting along better. I wanted him to spend the weekend with me.

Julian chuckled. "Please, it's the other way around."

He usually came over during the week when Mom went to church, but I hadn't seen him outside of school much. His mom had been too busy to bring him over and the buses that came by my house didn't run late. He'd taken a cab a couple times.

"You the only one always busy. Plus you know I been getting more hours at the skating rink. All I do is work."

"I know … but I miss you."

"I miss you too, we gon' get together."

I leaned further into the couch with the phone resting against my face.

"Tiffany?"

I yawned. "Hmm?"

"Promise me you ain't gon' do nothing crazy this weekend."

I stretched my arms over my head. "I won't."

"I'm serious. I don't want to hear about you and your friends clowning. You staying at Tori's house after y'all have that party, right?"

"She lives around the corner, babe. Either she's staying at my house or I'm staying at hers."

"Alright man, I'm serious."

"Me too. Call when you get out of work Friday

night. Maybe you can convince your mom to bring you over afterwards."

He hesitated. "We good?"

"Yeah, we're good."

"Alright, cool. I'mma try to come through. But either way I'mma make sure we spend time."

"Ok."

I hung up with Julian and dialed another number.

" 'Sup beautiful." Caine's deep voice filled my ear.

"So you're coming through this weekend?"

CHAPTER 17

"Heyyy, we're here to start a party!" Tori, Shonda, and Shae knocked on the door Friday after school.

"Heyyy! I'm ready." I held the door open.

"Heyyy, we finna get drunk." Shae stuttered.

"Oh my God," Shonda shook her head, handing me her jacket.

I laughed. "What's up, y'all."

"Alright," Tori handed me a stack of CDs. She walked past me into the kitchen. "What we need to do?"

Shae opened the cabinets over the stove. "What y'all got to eat? I'm hungry."

"You always hungry." Shonda teased.

"Shae, you can have some of them chips." I pointed to the sour cream and onion chips on the counter. I opened the refrigerator and took out the bags of party wings I'd let thaw. "We just gotta cook. Did you talk to Blaque and them about buying drinks?" I asked Tori.

"Yup," She washed her hands. "They're coming later."

We seasoned the chicken and talked over music.

"Hey boo," Julian knocked on the open door. He stepped into the hallway. "What's up everybody?" He nodded to my friends.

"Hey Julian," Tori waved. She knocked flour off her hands and wiped them in a towel.

"What's up bae," I gave Julian a hug.

"Just came to see what's up with you." He looked around the house. "Where the rest of your girls at?"

"They'll be here, they're coming later." I locked my hand in his. "How'd you get here?"

"You know I had to check on my baby. I had my man swing me by…"

Curtis came into the house behind Julian, flipping his keys around his finger.

"Hey Curtis," I waved.

"What's up."

"You coming back tonight?"

He glanced around the kitchen. "For what? Y'all said the party was tomorrow night."

"It is. We're playing cards later though."

"Okay," Curtis rubbed his hands together, looking over the pot Tori was warming up grease in. "*And y'all frying chicken? Let me get some.*"

I laughed. "It ain't done yet. You gotta come back."

"Fa sho," Curtis threw his head up. "Me and my brother will probably come back by. I gotta see what he wants to do."

Julian pulled me close and put his hands in my back pockets. "Look at you."

"What?" I tipped my head to the side.

"You…" He narrowed his eyes and ran his thumb across my chin. "You're so pretty, man."

I leaned my head on his shoulder. He was wearing my favorite cologne. It smelled like leather and sandalwood. "Thanks babe…"

Julian moved my hips to the song. He rapped a couple bars and kissed my cheek. "Alright," He squeezed my hand. "I can't stay, I just came to give you a kiss before I had to go to work."

"*Julian…*"

"I know boo," He leaned his face against mine.

"I want you to stay ... it won't be fun without you here."

"Don't act like that. We'll go out on Sunday, I promise."

"You're not gonna come back?"

"I'll try. But it's not looking good. You know how Moms is about me coming over here too late."

"Alright," I gave him a peck on the cheek. "Have a good night, call me when you get off."

"You too." He winked. "Be good, ok?"

"Bye, babe."

"Alright everybody," Julian turned to my girls. "I'mma check y'all out later," he snapped. "One."

"Bye Julian..." My friends waved.

"Alright Julian, we'll see you later!" Tori peeked head out of the kitchen. She waved over her head. "One."

Julian laughed as he pulled the door shut.

"Aww!" Tori dropped a batch of chicken in the grease. "Tiff, that boy is *sprung* ..."

"No he isn't," I giggled.

Shonda groaned. "Uggh…"

"What's your new friend's name?" Tori raised an eyebrow. "Caine? He's coming over later, right?"

"Girl yeah," I took a drink of my soda. "He said he'd stop by, we'll see though." It was hard to pin Caine down. He was always making a run.

"Mmm-mm-mm…" Shonda shook her head.

"*What* Shonda!"

She looked through the cabinet. "You're doing way too much, sister."

"I'm not doing anything," I held my hands out, "For real this time, Caine's just a friend."

"Yeah, okay."

Brianne came through the door 30 minutes later, "Hey ya'll, I'm here!"

"We know," Shonda teased, "With your big ol' mouth."

We were going back and forth between frying chicken and running into the living room when a new song came on. We clapped the beat for each other while we took turns dancing.

"Y'all are a mess," Brianne laughed at me and Tori.

"Y'all know y'all can't dance."

Brianne was short with paper bag skin and long black hair that touched the middle of her back. The guys from Camelot called her little Pocahontas. We teased her because she had so much hair, but wore it up in a bun every day. And because her mom was always telling her to get in the house. Her mom didn't play. She made sure Brianne and her little brother and sister went to church every week.

"Uh-uh," I said, "Don't laugh, I already know I'm stiff!" Dancing was one thing my girls messed with me about. They said I was the only black girl they knew who couldn't dance.

"Alright sister," Shonda came up next to me. "I'mma teach you."

"Shondaaaaa…"

"Come on, Tiffany," Shonda said, cracking up.

"We try this every time." Shonda tried to teach me how to dance whenever we had a party. "I'm good," I rocked, waving one hand in the air. "Let me keep doing what I'm doing."

"All you gotta do is this…" Shonda clasped her hands over her head and rolled her hips to the ground, dropped sensually and brought it back up.

"Girl please," I fell out on the sofa. "Shonda, you know I can't do that!"

"Wait," Tori two-stepped around the room, protecting the drink. "Look Shonda, I think I got it!"

"Girl," Brianne nudged her. "You ain't doin' nothing but swaying!"

"Hey...hey..." Tori snapped. "Hey...hey..."

"Get up Tiff," Shonda pulled me to my feet. "You can do it."

"— Get up!" Brianne teased.

"Fine." I got up off the couch. "Like this?" I put my hands on my hips and tried to roll like Shonda.

"Yeah," She said. "Now stop being so stiff!"

I widened my stance and worked my way down.

"Get it Tiffany!" Tori came next to me and joined in with Shae and Brianne. "Hey, hey..."

"See, y'all got it," Shonda said, "Ok, see if you can do this." She did a Jamaican style dance, slid into the splits, and popped on the floor.

"Aww shoot," Tori put her fist over her mouth.

"Hell naw," I threw my hand at Shonda, "You the *only* one that can do that."

We fell out laughing and went back to cooking. An hour later our boys from Camelot came with cards and liquor. They brought Mudslide for me. Tori said she hated it. She said she wasn't getting drunk off chocolate milk and liquor. We played spades like old men did at family reunions. Tori was my partner first. We slapped our cards on the table and yelled when we had a good hand. Shonda took over when Tori started drinking. Kendra and her best friend, Amber, came with a group of people around 11 o'clock. We moved the card table out of the way to make room.

CHAPTER 18

"Get your girl," I nudged Tori, cracking up. Shae was dancing in the middle of the living room. A bunch of guys were cheering her on.

"Aww shoot, go Shae!" Tori held her drink up.

"Heyyy, heyyy..." Shae swayed back and forth, pulling her shirt up and down to the music.

Shonda shook her head. "This heifer…" She rolled her eyes. "Shae, sit down somewhere."

"Naw," Tori laughed, "She's having fun, Shonda." We had always been kinda mean to Shae. She was the type of friend who stuck around no matter how you treated her. She would do whatever we asked, like go to the gas station to get us snacks when we didn't feel like walking. One time Tori and I had her walk all the way to the mall and back, twice, just to get us a dress to wear out that weekend.

"Go Shae," I took a sip of my drink and stumbled through the living room. The house was packed — guys Kendra knew from the city had showed up from out of nowhere. I went into the kitchen and got a piece of chicken off a greasy plate on the back of the stove.

"It's not done, baby."

"What?" I turned around to see Blaque.

"Hey Blaque, when'd you get here?" He had a 40 in one hand and a pint of liquor in the other.

"Just now. Me and my boys..." He hugged me from behind. "The chicken ain't finished."

"Oops." I giggled. I put my piece back in the grease and flipped the last batch. I braced myself against the counter. My head was swimming. The other thing my girls teased me about was being a lightweight. That used to be what they called Tori, but now she could hold liquor.

"You alright?"

"Yeah, I'm good." I took in Blaque's beautiful dark skin. He had on a blue Polo and a fitted hat.

He screwed the top off his 40. "...In here, drunk already."

I laughed. "No, I'm not."

He poured himself a drink. "Yeah, ok. Don't drink too much, beautiful."

"Alright now, Shae," Tori yelled from the living room. "Get it!"

I pushed away the fog that was clouding my thoughts and staggered back into the living room. The space was dim with just the corner lamp on. "What in the world is she doing?" I leaned against Tori.

"Heyyy, heyyy..." Shae unzipped her halter top to the beat.

I turned around. "I'm for real y'all, get Shae. She's trippin'."

"I got her," A brown-skinned guy pulled Shae into his arms. "Come on baby, come chill with me."

"*What?*" Tori looked at me and burst out laughing. "Shae's gettin' 'em!" She pulled my arm down and whispered. "You know who that is, right?"

I looked at her, confused.

"Girl, that's Benny. Who invited him?"

"Who is Benny?"

"*Benny.*" Her eyes lit up. "You know, Benny that used to go to Ottawa. The one I used to tell you about."

Benny was fine. Clean. He looked like the type that never had a girlfriend because he was too into himself. Like he would only talk to Shae because she'd been drinking.

Tori had told me all about him. He was like Caine. He pushed weight.

I wonder who told him about my party.

We turned the music up louder and Shae and Benny disappeared. The living room got more crowded as people showed up. The liquor took my stiffness away. I closed my eyes and worked my hips like Shonda. I felt bad for not checking on Shae, but I was too drunk to care.

I looked up after midnight and my eyes met Caine's.

Shit.

His dark eyes examined the room. He had on a wheat-colored Nautica vest, dark jeans, and matching Tims. His presence took my breath away.

"Come here," he mouthed. He stood in the doorway with Deacon and his cousins. I motioned for him to follow me upstairs.

"We can go in here." I nodded towards mom's room since Shae was in mine with Benny.

"Sup beautiful." Caine nudged the door shut.

"Hey," I blushed.

"Y'all having fun, huh? This ain't no card party."

"I know," I leaned into his chest to keep myself steady. "I don't know where all these people came from. I didn't invite them." I giggled. "I don't know why they're here."

"You alright?"

"Hmmm?"

"I said, you alright?"

I put my arms around Caine's shoulders. I was dizzy. "Yup."

I thought about all the times I had said "no," to Caine, but meant "yes." Julian had called an hour before to let me know he was off work. He wanted to come back over, but he had to work early the next day. Plus his mom wasn't feeling it. The tug on my heart was back.

"It's all good..." Caine whispered, "Don't worry 'bout them. I'mma stay with you tonight."

"Hmm?" I could have fallen over, the way the room was spinning.

"You ain't hear me?"

I caught myself from stumbling. "Uh-uh…"

Caine cupped my chin and pulled me closer. "I'm staying with you tonight."

He pulled my shirt up over my head and kissed me.

CHAPTER 19

"Hey sister," Shonda called early Saturday morning. "What's up, sister?" I giggled. I wrapped the cord around my waist and stepped into the kitchen. "Just calling to see who all is still there."

I whispered. "A few people are still 'sleep in the living room. Caine and them *just* left. What time did you end up leaving?"

"Like 7 this morning, y'all were still knocked out."

"I know. I just woke up. Can you believe all those people came through? And did you see Benny was here? Girl, tonight's party is gon' be *crazy*. We gotta—"

"Tiffany." Shonda cut me off.

"What?"

She held the phone, not saying anything.

"What's wrong?"

"I told my mom about last night."

"Shonda!"

"Uh-uh, don't 'Shonda' me."

"What are you talking about…why'd you tell?"

"Tiffany, you are out of control."

I stopped searching the refrigerator for breakfast so I could hear what she had to say.

"You got men we hardly know all over your mom's house. We don't know half those people in your living room right now … and them dudes from Flint?"

"What about them?"

"They are crazy!"

"No they're not, those are Kendra's boys—"

"I don't care whose boys they are. You gon' mess around and get hurt foolin' with them." First Julian, now Shonda. I didn't know what she was talking about. She didn't know anything about Caine and his cousins. I hadn't told her about Deacon getting taken. "Tiff, you need to calm down."

"Shonda—"

"I'm serious, sister, you're doing too much."

"Dang Shonda, you told your mom? What she say?"

"You really wanna know?"

"Yeah."

"She said if you was her child, she would beat yo' tail." We both cracked up.

"Your mom is crazy," I said, "I can hear her saying it, too."

"Mmmhmm, she might tell your mom, and you know she wasn't playing. I'm not coming back over there tonight, and you better call that party off."

"Shonda!"

"I'm serious, Tiffany. You need to slow down or something bad is gonna happen, I can feel it."

"Uggh."

I hung up the phone and dialed Tori's number.

"You up already?" She snickered. "I thought you'd still be knocked out."

"Yeah … I'm up."

"Why you sound like that? We had some fun last night. And did you see Shae pull Benny—"

"You talk to Shonda yet?"

"Naw, why?"

"She told her mom."

"Whaaat…?"

"She told about the party *and* about Caine and them staying the night."

"Are you serious?"

"Yeah. What is wrong with her? Shonda get on my nerves sometimes."

"Aww, Tiff … she told Ms. Tina?"

"Yup."

Shonda's mom was only in her thirties, but she fussed at us about how to act like she was a granny. She'd had Shonda young, so she would talk to us about not getting pregnant too soon and about life. She didn't want the same thing happening to us.

"Dang, Tiff. Okay, think … think … think…" I could hear Tori tapping on the receiver in the background. "You think Ms. Tina will tell?"

"I don't know. You know how she is … she can be cool sometimes. It just depends on if she's still trippin' by the time my mom gets back."

"Man, and that's in what, two days?"

"I know."

"Well, ain't no point in worrying about it now. We done already had the party. At least we had fun!"

"You so stupid."

"Hey, it's the truth."

"I can't believe she told her mom."

"That's Shonda for you," Tori chuckled. "But she is kinda right, Tiff."

"What makes you say that?"

"You got a lot going on. You do need to chill out a little."

I sucked my teeth. I was getting tired of everyone telling me I had a lot going on.

"Don't get mad sister." Tori said, lightly. "What was up with Caine last night?"

"You already know."

"Mmm-mm-mm…"

"What?"

"Come on now, Tiff. You don't think you need to slow down, just a little bit? We're just looking out for you."

I didn't say anything. Tori was usually down for the guys I was kicking it with. I wasn't used to her taking Shonda's side.

"Aye man, for real though? My mom said for you to stay the night over here."

"Are you serious?" I covered my head with my hand. I felt like the world was closing in on me. "She knows, too?"

"Not really. She just said she'd be more comfortable with you over here."

I took a deep breath and sighed. "Alright…"

"You talk to Julian?"

"Not yet. He worked late … he'll be calling soon though."

"Get ready for him to trip, you know his boys saw you with Caine."

Shoot.

I was sloppy. Julian's friend, Curtis had come back with his brother and some other guys.

What was I thinking?

I didn't know what it was about Caine. Why I was

risking everything I had with Julian to be with him. My world was unravelling around me and it was my fault. Caine had money, but I wasn't after that. He was attractive, but I had a man. I loved Julian.

It must have been the high he gave me.

The intoxicating feeling I got when Caine was around. Knowing I shouldn't want him. That I could get caught up any second. I was addicted to the rush I got from being with him. Wanting Caine was making life difficult. Nothing I did made sense.

CHAPTER 20

"What the hell, Tiffany!"
"Don't trip babe, it's not like that —"
"What the hell is wrong with you? Not like what? Like what all my boys are saying?"

"Let me just tell you what happened —"

"Naw man, you had some dude in yo' house all night? Tiffany, are you crazy? You don't even care who sees you acting a fool!"

"Julian…" I started crying.

"Whatchu crying for? You don't care about nobody but yourself. I'm the one that should be crying!"

"It's not like that, I didn't mean for nothing to happen, I just —"

"I swear to God, man, I ain't *never* cheated on you. I've had the chance, but I've never wanted to."

"I know —"

"I've *never* cheated!"

I held onto the phone and cried.

"I've never done you wrong, and this is how you do me? Right in front of my boys?"

"Julian," I whispered.

"What?"

"I'm sorry."

"You sorry? I can't even believe you got the nerve to say that to me."

"I am sorry."

"What would have happened if my boys wasn't there? You wouldn't have told me. You got caught, now you're sorry." Julian went off for the next hour. If we weren't on the phone he would have spit in my face. I felt like dirt. Everything he was saying about me was right.

Why do I act like this?

"Pack your things and get out of that house, Tiffany. Go to Tori's house tonight, or I swear, I will never speak to you again."

***

"Tiff…"

The answering machine kicked in just as I was about to walk out the house.

"Tiffany."

I had called the party off and stopped answering the phone right after I talked to Julian that morning. People I didn't know were calling to check on the address for the party, checking to see what kind of liquor I wanted. I couldn't talk. All I wanted to do was go to sleep and act like the night before hadn't happened. Julian was mad at me. Shonda's mom thought I was a ho and she was probably going to tell on me. I was exhausted. I let all the calls go to the answering machine.

"Aye, Tiff. Pick up the phone … it's Caine."

I shut the door and ran back into the living room. "Hello?"

" 'Sup Tiff, I been calling you all day."

"Hey Caine."

"What's up with you? I was starting to think you was avoiding me."

"Nah, it's not like that."

"Yeah? That's good. I was just calling to check on you. I had fun with you last night."

My heart skipped a beat, remembering the night before. Caine had left my mind in a daze. That was before I'd talked to Julian. I'd packed a bag for the rest of the weekend and had the house clean by the time it started to get dark. I figured if I stopped answering the phone people would get the hint that the party was cancelled.

"I had fun, too."

"Yeah?" He said, "That's good, so what's up with tonight?"

I looked around the room. "Nothing..."

"You don't need a repeat of last night with all them folks in your house. Why don't you call the party off? I'll get you something to eat and we can chill. Just me and you."

I felt like crying. Everything inside me screamed, *"Let him come over..."* I wanted someone to come at me the way Caine did. I needed someone to love me the way Julian did. I didn't know what to do.

"I can't," I choked back tears. "I mean, I'm not going to be home."

Caine scoffed. "Where you gon' be?"

"I'm chillin' with my girl."

"I thought we made plans. You backing out?" His words cut. He had told me he was coming back earlier that morning.

Tori, the party, Julian. I had plans with everyone. I couldn't think.

"I can't keep messing with you…"

"Aww, so your little boyfriend got to you, huh? Spend a night with me, now you got a guilty conscience."

"It's not like that."

"Yeah, it is. I already asked you to be my girlfriend. I'm not gonna keep asking you."

Tears threatened to spill down my cheeks. I didn't want Caine that bad, did I? I knew I wasn't the only girl he was dealing with. I couldn't be crying over him. I was losing control.

Shonda's voice came to my mind. *Those guys from Flint are dangerous…* What did she mean, "dangerous"? Like I was gonna die? I felt like death. I was exhausted. I was tired of lying. I was tired of sleeping with so many different people. I was tired of hanging out late. I wanted to go to sleep and wake up different.

"I'm not gonna be with you, Caine. Goodbye."

I hung up the phone and let the tears I'd been holding back slide down my face. I felt like I'd been ripped in half. My heart going one way and my mind in another. I didn't want to let go of Caine, but I had to or Julian was going to leave me. I couldn't lose him on top of everything else that had gone wrong.

I shouldn't have slept with Caine. I couldn't be with him. All I got from dealing with Caine was regret. Just like with Gideon. I had been dealing with so many different guys, like I wanted to get caught. Being out in the open for Julian's friends to see was an adrenaline rush. I would come home and see if he was going to cuss me out about who had seen me. It had become a game. I wanted to see how many guys I could mess with and not get found out. For the first time, I felt bad and wanted to stop. And now Julian knew.

They're dangerous...

Julian would be getting off work soon. I had to make sure I was around when he called Tori's house. I turned off the lights, grabbed my bag and shut the door behind me.

CHAPTER 21

"Good Morning!"
"Hey Corrine."
Corrine came bopping down the aisle.
She sat across from me and Kendra.
"You guys wanna come to church with me this weekend?"
She dug through her bag and flipped her hair.

Kendra propped her knees on the seat. "No thanks."

"Awww, you guys would like it."

I sat back in my seat. I wasn't trying to go to church. My life was miserable. It was Monday morning, a week after the party. Going to church wasn't going to make things better. People thought I was lame for cancelling and not telling them why. Mom hadn't found out about the party, but Julian had been trippin' ever since. He didn't trust me and I couldn't blame him. Whenever we were around each other he acted like he hated me.

He'd stopped walking me to class at school. He hardly called, and if he did, he'd go off about me cheating. A giant hole was growing in my heart. My world was crumbling. If he left me I didn't know what I would do.

"Come on you guys, you should come with me."

"No thanks."

I looked at Corrine, thinking about the past couple months. Her reputation. How could she be a ho?

***

"Hey Tiff!"

I looked around. I was at the mall trying to find something to wear to school the following day.

"Tiff! Over here!"

I looked across the food court and saw Corrine waving from McDonalds.

"Hey girl," I walked across the atrium and hugged her.

"Hey!" She squeezed me tight.

"You been working here long?"

"Just a couple months. I told you guys to come and I'd hook you up. You want something to eat?"

I laughed. "Sure." I placed my order and she prepared it. I stood by her register eating my food.

"Yeah girl, my mom is crazy. She had me get up in the middle of the night to vacuum. Talking 'bout, I should have done all my chores like she said. I was like, *'Dang ma, I forgot.'* She said, *'I don't care about you forgetting, get up!'*" Corrine snapped her fingers. " *'Get to it.'* Girl. That's them Puerto Ricans for you."

I laughed. I tried to act normal even though my world was falling apart all around me.

"...Oh, my goodness. One time, do you know what my sister gon' say?"

" — Corrine?"

"What?" She walked around the register bay with a towel.

"Can I ask you something?"

"Yeah."

"Why you always talking about church?"

She stopped by a table and wiped crumbs to the floor. "Because, I love God." Her curls bounced. "I used to be a mess. I was crazy last year. If you had known me then…" She shook her head. "But I started going to church and everything's different. I talk about church so much because I love my relationship with God." She grabbed wrappers off the table and moved to the next section.

I stood there, looking across the food court. *Everything's different...*

Different how? That didn't make sense to me. From the things I had heard about Corrine she was like two different people. How could she go from acting like a ho to being Miss Perfect in one semester?

I threw away my food.

That was the first time I had ever heard Corrine bring up her past. I wished she wasn't at work so she could tell me more.

***

"Hello?"

"Come out."

My heart jolted at the sound of Caine's voice.

"Hellooo," I sang into the phone like I didn't recognize his deep timbre.

"You know who this is, don't play," he said. His voice sounded ragged from how late it was. "Come through."

"Where?"

"To the room."

"I *can't* Caine." My belly did flips.

"Yes you can."

"You know I gotta boyfriend."

"I don't wanna hear about that dude, I wanna chill with you tonight." I could picture Caine's face frowning up. He hated when I talked about Julian.

"Mmmm…"

"What you humming for?" He blew smoke into the receiver. "You wanna see me too."

"It's nothing, I'm just listening to you talk."

"How you been?" He switched gears. "Whatchu been up to?"

"Going to school. Same ol' stuff." It had been weeks since I'd spoken to him. We hadn't talked since I cancelled on him after the party.

"You seen Kendra lately? Me and Johnny was supposed to kick it with her and Amber and they little friends last weekend."

I sat up. I hadn't heard anything about Kendra and Caine hanging out.

"…I guess them plans fell through."

I played with the fringe on my blanket. "We haven't been out nowhere, but I see Kendra at school every day."

"Still gettin' them A's?"

I smiled. "Something like that."

He chuckled. "That's good. I knew you was smart as hell, I like that about you..." Voices picked up around him, I could hear his cousins kickin' it in the background. "So what's up, you ready to quit trippin'?"

I cradled the phone against my shoulder and drew my knees up close.

"I'm not trippin'..." I said, voice barely above a whisper. Mom had gone to bed early, but something in my chest told me not to talk loud.

"Come through then, it's been too long since I've seen you."

"Where?"

"Don't worry about all that, just come."

Say no...

I bit at the corner of my lip. The sound of Caine's voice and the chill that ran up my spine made me nervous. Scared. I did miss him.

Say no...

What was wrong with me? I tried to quiet the tug on my heart. I wasn't afraid of Caine himself. He had never done anything bad to me. What was I scared of? The way I'd played Julian must have given me a guilty conscience.

Julian ain't perfect, I argued with myself. I'd been hearing things about him talking to other girls for the past few weeks.

"I gotta go to school tomorrow Caine," I twisted around to look at the clock on the microwave, "it's like, 11 o'clock at night."

"You'll be back in time to go to school."

I didn't say anything. I knew Caine wasn't good for me. But something about him drew me in. Julian was mad and everything was falling apart around me. I didn't want to make things worse. I had to be better. I was trying to heal my heart. I wanted love; I wanted someone to fix the pain I'd been feeling since I was younger. All Caine could do was take.

"Say you comin' through..."

Caine put people on, people answered to him, he was used to getting what he wanted. I knew I shouldn't, but I wanted him to want me. What he could give me wasn't real, but it felt good when he was around. Even though my heart was with Julian.

"I'mma call you a cab. I'll see you in an hour."

"Nooo, I really can't."

"I don't know why you playin', you already know you coming."

I glanced at the stairs. I did miss Caine, and Mom wouldn't know I left. I didn't have to stay long. I let out the breath I'd been holding.

"Okay..."

"That's what I'm talking about. I'mma see you when you get here."

Click.

My fingers hovered over the dial pad while I tried to decide if I was going to call Caine back and tell him I couldn't come. I pulled my legs tighter into my chest.

I'll be back before morning, nobody will know.

I put the phone down and tip-toed upstairs to get dressed.

***

I pulled the front door shut and locked it, trying to muffle the scraping noise it made after it rained and the wood swelled up tighter than the metal. I waited a few seconds to see if mom's light would pop on. I looked up at her window.

Nothing.

I counted to five in my head, then ran to the waiting cab.

AFTERWORD

Hey you guys! Thank you so much for reading the second installment of Restore. If you're wondering what's going to happen you won't be disappointed. It's about to get real!

If you recall, book one had several heavy themes. One of the biggest was sexual assault. In this book the biggest overall theme is the aftermath of trauma. A lot of times we go through things as kids and young adults and never deal with it.

We stuff down our traumatic experiences and keep it moving like nothing happened.

At this point in Restore I'd stuffed down a whole lifetime of events. Getting kidnapped, my parents' devastating separation and divorce, sexual assaults, and the resulting toxic relationship with Gideon.

Sometimes we think we've gotten over our past, but

the trauma shows up in our actions. You can tell how much Gideon affected me by how I rationalized the things I did. I considered him and how he would act in different situations I faced instead of what I should have known to be right.

This isn't healthy.

I compared my relationships to the abusive, dysfunctional situation I had with Gideon in order to figure out which direction to take. I didn't have a focal point for "good" anymore. I was in a toxic relationship with myself and everyone around me. I wasn't healthy and it was getting dangerous.

The biggest takeaway I want you to get from this book is to get help when you need it. Don't wait for life to spiral out of control before you reach out for help. If you find yourself in a toxic situation utilize every resource you can find to figure out your next step.

If you're overcoming trauma here's what I would do.

Admit it to yourself.

Sometimes acknowledging what you've been through is half the battle. If you've gone through something traumatic sometimes you just need to admit it to yourself before you can move forward. Own what happened to you. Acknowledge it. Journal about it. Tell yourself the truth.

Go to therapy.

We often stigmatize therapy, but it's an important part of the healing process. Talking your issues over with a professional can give you the insight and clarity you need for a fresh start. Don't be afraid to reach out for help

Pray.

There's power in prayer. God loves you and wants to protect you from anything that would harm you. Prayer is giving God an invitation into your life. It allows Him to access what hurt you and opens the door to Him to help you heal.

Whelp, here we are at the end. There's so much I wanted to share with you I decided to split Restore into four books. Book three is coming soon! In the meantime connect with me on social media. You can find me on Instagram @Author_Tiffany_Dionne, and on Facebook at "Tiffany Dionne." Follow me for updates on what's going on in my life, speaking engagements, and new books. Send me a message, I'd love to hear from you!!

Last but not least, please leave a review on Amazon and your favorite booksellers sites. It helps readers like you find my books.

I love you and I appreciate you!!

Tiff